GEOPOLYMPICS
The Great Geopolitical Stories of the Olympic Games

Kévin Veyssière

GEOPOLYMPICS
The Great Geopolitical Stories
of the Olympic Games

Max Milo

Max Milo, Paris, 2024

www.maxmilo.com

ISBN : 978-2-31502-178-9

Introduction

The Paris Olympic Games promise to be the highlight of 2024, both in sporting and geopolitical terms. They are taking place in a particular context, marked by the war between Russia and Ukraine, as well as the resumption of the Israeli-Palestinian conflict at high intensity. These events are bound to feature on the Olympic agenda, given the close links between sport and politics. The Games are more than just an international sporting event; they are also one of the arenas of global geopolitics. Since the beginning of the 21st century, the IOC (International Olympic Committee) has brought together more than 10,000 athletes and 206 national delegations (the NOCs) for the Games—more than the UN and its 193 member states. The Olympics are watched by nearly 5 billion television viewers, making them the world's most-watched media and sporting event. In a word: unmissable...

The Olympic Games have long been a reflection of international relations. Since their rebirth in Athens in 1896, each edition has mirrored the political, economic and social issues of its era. Far from being mere sporting confrontations between athletes, the Olympic Games have always been the setting for demonstrations of power, identity claims and diplomatic attempts. Thus, from the very first modern Games, the new Greek state drew on its reserves to use the event to legitimize its new-found greatness in the eyes of the world.

And yet, this great sporting gathering, the brainchild of its "founding father", Baron Pierre de Coubertin, had to be above all politically neutral in order to pursue a certain ideal of peace and universalism. However, the further back in time the Games go, the more they become part of the geopolitical fabric of their time. As in the case of the 1920 Antwerp Games, where the "losers" of the Great War—led by Germany—were simply not invited.

In fact, it was only a few years later, in Germany, that the Olympic Games became a means of political instrumentalization for the first time, without any intervention from the IOC. The 1936 Berlin Games were a veritable propaganda tool for Hitler's regime, promoting the illusory image of a powerful and peaceful Germany... while masking the darker abuses of his dictatorship. After the Second World War, the Olympics became an extension of the Cold War, with the two superpowers, the Soviet Union and the United States, using the sporting arena as a battleground. The number of medals and the final rankings were part of the struggle for influence between the Western and Eastern blocs. This rivalry came to a head with the reciprocal boycotts of Moscow in 1980 and Los Angeles in 1984.

The use of mass boycotts is nothing new. In 1976, at the Montreal Games, 25 African countries had already decided to withdraw from the Olympiad to protest against the participation of New Zealand, whose rugby team had played in South Africa, then under the apartheid regime. In terms of societal demands, the 1968 Olympics in Mexico City were also a historic platform for protest against racial segregation policies. The raised, black-gloved fists of American athletes Tommie Smith and John Carlos are the emblematic sign, which has since been widely used in the fight against racism and social injustice.

The Olympics are also a formidable revealer for nations, particularly those that have recently gained their independence. The post-World War II editions in particular embody this with the decolonization process in Africa, Asia and Oceania. This was also the case in Barcelona in 1992, which marked the end of the Cold War and the integration of new countries into the Olympic world. This recognition is all the more political given the media coverage the Olympics have gained over the decades, especially the opening ceremony, which has a strong symbolic value thanks to the Parade of Nations. The battle for Chinese representation between China and Taiwan, the IOC's recognition of Palestine in 1996 and Kosovo's participation in the 2016 Olympics, whose independence is disputed, are all cases that testify to the importance of being part of the Olympic community.

If, in the traditional Olympic spirit, "the important thing is to take part", certain states are using the Olympic Games to implement a real political strategy to win and capture Olympic performances. This is evident in the medal table, where the battle between China and the United States has replaced the American-Soviet duel. But the competition is also being played out in the organization and hosting of the Olympics. On the one hand, this mega-event offers host countries an unrivalled global platform for displaying their economic, cultural and organizational power. Like other major sporting events, such as the soccer World Cup, the Olympics are a veritable tool for promoting "national branding". On the other hand, the Olympic Games enable states to enhance their international image and strengthen their *soft power,* *i.e.* their ability to influence others through attraction and persuasion rather than coercion.

By voting and choosing the "host country", the IOC has a major political impact. Especially since, in a bid to achieve universalism, move beyond its Western heritage and economically develop its flagship event, the Olympic body is opening up the Games to new horizons. This may be in line with the strategy of new emerging powers, for whom organizing the Olympic Games is a way of demonstrating their modernity. This was illustrated by the 2008 Beijing Olympics, when China blew the budget for an Olympiad, spending $42 billion to stage an event capable of demonstrating its power. Emerging powers then followed suit (Russia with Sochi in 2014, Brazil with Rio in 2016) and other ambitious countries are beginning to position themselves for future editions, such as Qatar, Saudi Arabia and India.

All these new challenges make Paris 2024 a major political challenge for France. The aim is to demonstrate its ability to organize and host major international events, while presenting the world with model Games in terms of budgetary control and sustainable development. However, the preparation of these Games will be subject to major security risks, exacerbated by the current geopolitical context. The delegations from Israel, Palestine, Ukraine and Russia (under a neutral banner) will be under particular scrutiny, as these Olympic delegations are seen as an extension of their countries.

This book invites sports fans, geography buffs and the simply curious to explore the history of our world through the Olympic Games, from the end of the 19th century to the present day. Each pedagogically concise chapter reveals the most striking geopolitical backdrops surrounding each edition of the Olympic Games, helping us to better understand why the Games are more than just sport, and why they can be analyzed as a theater of nations, where sporting performances and power games are intertwined.

Kévin Veyssière

Chapter 1: The Geopolitical Origins of the Olympic Games

The Olympic Games were reintroduced in Athens in 1896 thanks to the determination of one man: Baron Pierre de Coubertin. Although the reintroduction of the Olympiads was a private initiative, it was nevertheless part of a geopolitical context, making the modern Games a political construction from the outset. To better understand this, we need to go back to the beginning of the 19th century. The world was undergoing major social, economic and cultural upheaval. The Industrial Revolution, which began in the UK and spread to Europe, North America and Asia, accelerated technological innovations such as the steam engine and the telegraph, which revolutionized transport and communication, facilitating international trade and colonial expansion. It was also a period of major transformation, marked by the rise of nationalism and the consolidation of nation-states. These new, unified or consolidated political entities, armed with a strong national identity and a flourishing industrial economy, sought to extend their influence to secure their resources, markets and strategic territories. The result is imperialist competition for a share of the planet.

The British, French, German, Russian and Ottoman empires were engaged in a fierce battle for control of the world's main strategic nodes. These rivalries gave rise to numerous direct and indirect conflicts, including one that played a major role in the (re)introduction of the Olympic Games: the Franco-Prussian War (1870-1871). France was defeated, and its severe defeat profoundly weakened the country both politically and economically. Worse still, it seriously undermined national pride. Some observers attributed this failure to the supposed physical weakness of the French population compared to that of Prussia, the future Germany. A perception that strongly influenced Pierre de Coubertin.

British Influence in the Reintroduction of the Games

This French aristocrat is convinced that physical education is essential to the personal development of individuals. In particular, for the younger generation to develop their physical and mental health and become responsible citizens. This conviction was shared by Prussia, his rival at the time, who was already integrating gymnastics into its educational system, illustrating the importance of sport in strengthening the individual and, in a broader perspective, the nation's armed body.

However, the most inspiring educational model through sport at the time was that of the British Empire[1]. Soccer and rugby, codified in the 1860s and 1870s respectively, became symbols of this model. Born within the confines of elitist British *public schools,* these educational practices were used to instruct, channel and socialize pupils.

---

1. TERRET Thierry, *Histoire du sport,* PUF, coll. Que sais-je?, 2013.

They quickly gained in popularity, their rules being formalized and disseminated far beyond the borders of the British Empire. This contributed to reinforcing the United Kingdom's influence through this sporting and social practice, accentuating the influence of the world's leading power at the time.

Influenced by this British approach to sport, Pierre de Coubertin undertook several trips to the UK in the 1880s, exploring the educational and sporting system that prevailed there. It was during these visits that he met a figure who was to exert a decisive influence on his thinking: Dr. William Penny Brookes. A doctor and educator in Much Wenlock, Brookes was a pioneer in the promotion of physical education in England. He is best known for founding the "Wenlock Olympics" in 1850, an annual sporting competition designed to encourage physical exercise among young people and adults in his area. These games, which included a variety of sporting events from running to high jumping to archery, had a direct impact on Coubertin. He was particularly taken by the spirit of these competitions, which emphasized fair play and the importance of amateurism. These were "noble" principles that he would later seek to integrate into the very heart of modern Olympic philosophy.

The Rebirth of Greece and Olympia

The interest in reintroducing such "Olympiads" is not insignificant. It was part of a wider movement in the 19th century to reappropriate the heritage of ancient Greece. The independence of the Greek state in 1832[2] led to an infatuation with the culture and

---

2. We'll come back to this at greater length in Chapter 2.

history of antiquity. Against this backdrop of renewed fascination, Greek philanthropist Evangelis Zappas embarked on an ambitious project: the reintroduction of the ancient Olympic Games. These Games were a series of sporting competitions between representatives of the Greek city-states, and were one of the Panhellenic Games of ancient Greece. They were first held in 779 BC in the city of Olympia. These major events of ancient Greece attracted athletes from all regions of the Greek world in a variety of disciplines, including running, wrestling, javelin and discus throwing, as well as the pentathlon. These competitions, beyond their sporting aspect, fulfilled an essential function of diplomacy and peace, materialized through the "Olympic Truce". This meant suspending part of the hostilities to ensure the safety of participants and spectators. It was from 393 AD onwards that the Games gradually disappeared, when the Roman emperor Theodosius ordered the abandonment of ancient Greek places of worship. Inspired by this legacy, the "Zappas Olympics" were held in Athens in 1859, 1870 and 1875.

Parallel to these events, the city of Olympia was awakened from its slumber between 1875 and 1881 by the teams of German archaeologist Ernst Curtius. Initiatives to revive the Games and the (re)discovery of the historic site revived interest in this age-old competition. Particularly for Pierre de Coubertin, who declared: "Long before I thought of extracting an innovative principle from its ruins, I had worked in spirit to rebuild, to revive its linear silhouette. Germany has succeeded in exhuming what remains of Olympia; why shouldn't France succeed in reconstituting its splendors?"[3]

---

3. COUBERTIN Pierre de, *Les batailles de l'éducation physique. Une campagne de vingt-et-un ans,* Paris, Librairie de l'Éducation physique, 1909.

This declaration reveals Pierre de Coubertin's threefold aim in reviving the Olympic Games. Firstly, sporting competitions could be a powerful diplomatic means of fostering peace and international understanding between peoples at a time when nation-states were coming into being. Secondly, these competitions can serve an educational purpose, by putting "noble" values such as surpassing oneself and fair play back at the heart of the game. Finally, sport can help revitalize the French national spirit, and put France back on track against its rivals on a terrain other than the military field.

The Sorbonne Congress of 1894: Coubertin's Successful French Diplomatic Venture

Coubertin undertook the difficult task of reviving the Olympic Games on an international scale. Difficult, because in a context where the means of communication and long-distance transport were still in their infancy, there were few events capable of bringing together the great international powers and peacefully showcasing the strengths of each. Except for events such as the Universal Exhibitions, which had the capacity to bring states together in a spirit of discovery and exchange, and to transcend divisions and borders.

Thanks to extensive preparatory work, conferences and his vast network of contacts in the fields of education, finance and sport, Pierre de Coubertin succeeded in bringing together 2,000 guests and, above all, 20 delegates from 13 foreign sports federations for the Sorbonne Congress from June 16 to 24, 1894. Coubertin's talent as an orator persuaded the delegates of the importance of his initiative. The Olympic movement and the renaissance of the Games were underway.

Several pioneering decisions were taken at the Congress[4] :

- the reintroduction of the Olympic Games every four years, thus resuming the frequency of the ancient Games;
- the creation of the International Olympic Committee (IOC), responsible for overseeing the organization of the Games;
- the adoption of the Olympic Charter, stressing the importance of personal development, excellence, education through sport, political neutrality and the contribution to a peaceful world through greater mutual understanding between peoples;
- amateurism, as a criterion for participation, prioritizing the «love» and «nobility» of sporting practice over the quest for financial gain.

All that remained to be decided was where the first Games would be held. Coubertin, a fervent patriot, proposed staging them at the same time as the Universal Exhibition in Paris in 1900. However, concerned that the six-year wait might dampen enthusiasm and public interest, the members of the Congress preferred to bring the date forward to 1896.

First Battle to Host the First Games

As the historic birthplace of the Games, Greece submits Athens' bid without delay. Against this backdrop of still-rare international events, the Greek bid was not the only one to emerge. The British Empire, with London, and the Austro-Hungarian Empire, with Budapest, also showed interest. These metropolises have many

---

4. Olympics.com, "Olympic Congress Paris 1894", IOC.

assets, backed by imperial power. But above all, these bids reveal a twofold intention: to seize the initiative of reintroducing the Olympic Games as an asset of power and, potentially, to eclipse the French rival by appropriating its project.

Not all of these proposals enjoy the unconditional support of all their governments. The British Empire, with its long tradition of national and international sporting events, was more interested in organizing Pan-British Games with its own sports, raising questions about the need for modern Olympic Games. The German Empire, for its part, remained notably absent from the Congress, thus avoiding direct confrontation with France, in the knowledge that Pierre de Coubertin would have done it no favours in any case.

At a time when the Olympic movement had barely begun, the first geopolitical negotiations were taking place behind the scenes. In this game, Athens' bid appeared to be the most favorable, especially as Coubertin supported the idea. After consulting Dimítrios Vikelas, who represented Greece, Coubertin proposed Athens, and quickly convinced the Congress of the historical and symbolic importance of the Greek capital as an extension of the ancient Games. On June 23, 1894, Athens' bid was officially accepted, and Vikelas was elected the first President of the IOC, marking the start of preparations for the first modern Olympic Games[5].

Greece had just two years to organize this unprecedented event. A choice which, as we shall see in the next chapter, was not only based on the Greek heritage of the Olympic Games, but was also motivated by political and nationalist considerations on the part of the nascent Greek state.

---

5. COUBERTIN Pierre de, *Olympic Memoirs*, Bartillat, 2016.

CHAPTER 2 - 1896 ATHENS: THE FIRST GAMES IN THE SERVICE OF THE NEW GREEK STATE

Greece has finally succeeded in being entrusted with the organization of the first modern Olympic Games. What could be more logical for the birthplace of the ancient Games? Yet this decision, while seemingly natural in view of its historical legitimacy, came at a delicate time. At the time, the Greek state was still seeking stability and full autonomy, and was seeking to forge its own identity on the international stage. Indeed, the country regained full independence in 1832 after a war with the Ottoman Empire (1821-1829), which was largely due to two external factors.

The first is that the Greek cause enjoyed strong support outside its borders, thanks to the development of a strong "philhellene" movement in Europe[6]. This movement, which emerged during the Enlightenment of the 18th century, placed the ideals of ancient Greece and its contributions to Western civilization on a pedestal. This period thus led to the emergence of a national consciousness

---

6. BOISSONADE Euloge, CHARPENTIER Henri, *La grande histoire des Jeux olympiques*, France Empire, 1999.

among Westernized Greek elites in the diaspora, creating international solidarity in favor of Greek liberation.

The second is that the European powers' support for Greek independence was also motivated by geopolitical considerations, notably the desire to weaken the strategic rival Ottoman Empire. For this reason, British, French and Russian forces were quick to join the Greek War of Independence. The combined fleet of the European powers led to a strategic victory in 1827 at the Battle of Navarin, marking a turning point in international support for the Greek cause.

However, the independence gained in 1832, although formally recognized, was in fact a limited independence, as Greece found itself under the direct influence of the great powers. The installation of a foreign monarch, King Otto of Bavaria, who became Otto I, and economic supervision by international entities symbolize this foreign stranglehold on the country's internal affairs. This foreign tutelage affected Greek domestic politics and national identity, exacerbating tensions between pro-Western elites and nationalist movements keen to preserve national authenticity and independence.

A Young Greek State Dependent on Foreign Powers

Although Greece was freed from the Ottoman Empire, it still faced numerous internal problems and interference from outside powers. Politically, the young kingdom was plagued by chronic instability. A popular uprising overthrew the monarch Othon I. But this did not prevent the British, French and Russian powers from maintaining their hold on Greek territory and installing Prince William of Denmark, who became George I "King of the Hellenes".

The new monarch was faced with an explosive situation. Greek nationalist agitation was very strong, and the "Great Idea"—in other words, the desire to unite all Greeks in a single country—was at the heart of national politics. The beginning of George I's reign was therefore marked by a territorial expansion of Greece, to calm nationalist ardor, even though the threat of the Ottoman Empire had not been averted.

The cost of this policy, coupled with the interference of foreign powers, led to major financial difficulties, characterized by excessive public spending, growing debt and structural weaknesses in the economy. Financial dependence on the great powers became even more pronounced with the public insolvency of 1893 and the establishment of an international financial commission to supervise Greek finances.

The Importance of Organizing the Olympic Games for a Diminished Kingdom of Greece

Greece's back was against the wall. However, the idea of reintroducing the Olympic Games, put forward by the Frenchman Pierre de Coubertin, was seen by the Greek royal authorities as a formidable means of reaffirming the full autonomy of their state, as well as reinvigorating Greek nationalism. This undoubtedly explains why Greece was more eager than other states to secure the organization of this first-ever Olympiad. The recent IOC decision to award the 1896 Games to Greece is a victory that goes far beyond sport for the country. It is an opportunity to demonstrate the country's determination in the face of adversity, to reinforce its international image and to mobilize its resources to overcome the political, military and economic obstacles that stand in its way towards stability.

However, at the end of 1894, the organizing committee headed by Stephanos Skouloudis presented a report indicating that the cost of the Games would be three times higher than expected, amounting to more than 3 million drachmas[7]. The committee, overwhelmed, resigned. A disaster for the early days of Olympism, when the Games were due to be reintroduced in less than two years' time. Thanks to the efforts of Pierre de Coubertin and Dimítrios Vikelas, the first (Greek) President of the IOC, a campaign was launched to keep the Olympic movement alive. The Kingdom of Greece did not want to let its chance slip either, and the royal family took up the torch. Crown Prince Constantine became President of the Organizing Committee, with the task of raising the funds needed to stage the Games. Relying on the patriotism of the Greek people, he succeeded in raising a large wave of financial contributions, while the sale of tickets and a special series of postage stamps completed the financing.

But it was above all thanks to George Averoff, an influential Greek businessman, that the organization of the Games was saved. He responded to Constantine's appeal by financing the restoration of the Panathenaic Stadium with a generous donation of 920,000 drachmas. In tribute to his major contribution, a statue of Averoff was erected and unveiled at the entrance to the stadium a few days before the start of the Games, where it remains to this day.

---

7. KOULOURI Christina, in *Une histoire mondiale de l'olympisme : 1896-2024*, Atlande, 2023.

Using the Games to Reaffirm Greece's Independence

On April 6, 1896, the restored Panathenaic Stadium, a symbol of Greece's ancient power, was transformed into a majestic theater for the opening ceremony, attracting, according to sources at the time, some 80,000 spectators. The 241 athletes, representing 12 nations (although some reports speak of 14), lined up on the field, symbolically uniting their respective countries in a historic moment. However, it's worth noting that women were banned from competing in these first Games, reflecting the norms of the time that limited their participation, including in the sporting arena.

After Prince Constantine's speech, it was indeed the King of Greece, George I, who officially opened the Games with these words: "I declare the opening of the first international Olympic Games in Athens. Long live the Nation. Long live the Greek people.[8] A speech that was already more political than it seemed, given the context of Greece's reaffirmation of its independence from outside powers. The date of April 6 was not chosen by chance, as it corresponds to March 25 in the Gregorian calendar, the same date as the Greek uprising against the Ottoman Empire in 1921. The Ottoman rival was the first country in Olympic history to refuse to participate, due to ongoing territorial and political tensions with Greece. The very first Olympic "boycott". There were other tensions on the sporting front, too, as French gymnasts refused to compete against their German rivals, reflecting the political rivalries between France and Germany.

---

8. WAWRZYNIAK Richard, *Histoire(s) des Jeux olympiques*, Mareuil Éditions, 2021.

This did not prevent all the events from going ahead smoothly. Greece was the big winner of this very first edition, with the highest number of "medals" (47). This figure should be put into perspective, however, as the Greek delegation was by far the largest, taking part on home soil, and transport constraints at the time meant that other countries were unable to bring such a large contingent. However, it was (already) the USA who officially dominated the "medals" table. The American delegation won the most titles, 11, while Greece took just 10. James Connolly, in the triple jump, became the first Olympic champion of the modern era, inaugurating the long list of American sporting legends to come. If the term medal is used here in quotation marks, it's because, contrary to future practice, the champions of 1896 received an olive wreath and a silver medal. The tradition of gold, silver and bronze medals only came later, at the 1904 Olympic Games in St. Louis.

Spyrídon Loúis: The First "National Hero" of the Games

The organization of these Games by Greece was made all the more special by one event. The dazzling victory of Spyrídon Loúis, then a simple shepherd, in the marathon event. This event was far from insignificant, as it symbolized the heritage of ancient Greece. This long-distance race was inspired by the legend of Philippides, the famous messenger of the battle of Marathon, and was reintroduced in these first Games at the suggestion of Coubertin's friend Michéal Bréal, to reinforce the ancient symbolism. Loúis, far from being the favorite, was the first to enter the Panathenaic Stadium, welcomed by a euphoric crowd. Crown Prince Constantine even ran the last lap with the eventual winner. Spyrídon Loúis's victory triggered wild celebrations, as described in the official report of the Games: "Here, the Olympic winner was received with all honors; the king rose from his seat and congratulated him most warmly on his success. Some of the king's aides-de-camp and several members of the committee went so far as to embrace the winner, who was finally carried in triumph into the retreat hall beneath the vaulted entrance. The scene that then unfolded inside the Stadion is not easy to describe; even foreigners were carried away by the general enthusiasm."[9]

An incredible scene then unfolded. Princes Constantine and George, themselves representatives of the Greek monarchy, take Spyrídon Loúis in their arms and carry him to King George I, standing before his marble throne. The shepherd became the national hero and, above all, the symbol of unity between the nation, the Greek people and the ruling royal family. Back in 1896, an Olympic champion became more than a sportsman: he became a "national hero", a standard-bearer for the entire nation thanks to his sporting achievements.

Greece was at the heart of this Olympic renaissance, and King George I himself was won over. Faced with the Greek national enthusiasm for the Games, he tried to persuade the Olympic movement that the Games should remain on Greek soil and be held every four years on home soil. However, Pierre de Coubertin was strongly opposed to this idea, as he considered international rotation to be one of the cornerstones of the modern Olympic Games as an international and peacemaking event. For the Greeks, the decision was seen as a deprivation of one of their greatest national treasures. The

---

9. LAMBROS Spyridon P. and POLITES Nikolas G., « Rapport officiel des Jeux olympiques de 1896 ».

Olympics are no longer a Greek monopoly. From now on, they will have a more "universal" aspect, being organized every four years in different countries. The next stage is eagerly awaited by the "father of the Games", Coubertin, since the 1900 edition will be held in Paris, France.

Chapter 3 - 1912 Stockholm - 1920 Antwerp: Impossible Olympic Neutrality

The first edition of the Olympic Games in 1896 was a successful challenge for Coubertin in his bid to revive Olympism. However, there was still a long way to go before the event was established as a major international event. It was time to confirm this success by organizing the next Games. But subsequent editions had a hard time establishing themselves. In Paris in 1900, the Games were overshadowed by the Universal Exhibition, struggling to attract the attention they deserved. Four years later, in St. Louis, USA, geographical remoteness and prohibitive participation costs considerably hampered the Games' international reach. Above all, this edition was marked by an indelible stain: the parallel holding of the "Anthropological Days", whose aim was to compare athletic skills between the "races", and which cast a shadow over the beginnings of Olympism[10].

In search of renewal, the IOC and Coubertin set about revitalizing the Games by organizing an intermediate edition in 1906

---

10. WERNICKE Luciano, *Les histoires insolites des Jeux olympiques d'été*, Amphora, 2020.

in Athens. This initiative remobilized the event and restored its credibility, a trend that was confirmed two years later at the 1908 London Games. However, this Olympiad was still backed by another event, the Trade Exhibition, commemorating the Entente Cordiale between the United Kingdom and France. The Olympic Games were still struggling to assert themselves fully in the face of the major world events of the day, underlining the imperative need to establish these Olympiads as an exclusive and distinct event.

Stockholm 1912: A High-Risk Parade of Nations

Sweden played a key role in this development. Few countries were in a hurry to submit their bid, via a city, to host the 1912 Olympic Games. Stockholm was the only one to submit a bid, and *de facto* took over the organization. Despite the lack of competition, King Gustav V did not hesitate to mobilize the Swedish state to underwrite a large part of the costs of organizing the Games, a significant investment for the time, amounting to 415,000 crowns[11]. A gamble given that, for the first time, no other event would be associated with the Games. However, the 5th Olympiad was a resounding success, attracting record participation from 28 countries. For the first time, athletes from all five continents took part (Japan for Asia, South Africa and Egypt for Africa, Australasia, a joint team from Australia and New Zealand, for Oceania), giving the Stockholm Games a universal aura. At least almost "universal", since this edition also reflected its patriarchal era and the misogynistic

---

11. Thilou Thomas, *Histoire(s) de Jeux : Les Jeux Olympiques de 1896 à 2021, 125 ans d'Humanité*, L'Harmattan, 2022.

vision of Pierre de Coubertin, and brought together just 48 women out of the 2,408 athletes present.

The Games also gave a new dimension to the Parade of Nations, first introduced in 1908. Initially intended as a means of showcasing athletes in their national colors and reflecting a spirit of fraternity that crossed borders, this parade of symbols took on an entirely different meaning in Sweden. It took place at a time of strong nationalist demands from the major powers, foreshadowing the upheavals of the First World War. Finland, still part of the Russian Empire, marched under its own flag, asserting its desire for autonomy and a distinct national identity. The Austrian and Hungarian delegations marched separately, even though they belonged to the same state. Similarly, Serbia's participation in the 1912 Games coincided with a period of high tension in the Balkan region, marked by the Balkan Wars (1912-1913). These conflicts saw Serbia and other Balkan states fight the Ottoman Empire for independence. This impetus for national affirmation, in the sporting context of the Olympic Games, resonated with the geopolitical tensions that were soon to set Europe ablaze.

Berlin 1916: The 6th "Ghost" Olympic Games

The transition from this quest for national identity and sovereignty, manifested at the 1912 Games, to the upsurge of larger-scale conflicts, was echoed on June 28, 1914 in Sarajevo. On that day, Crown Prince Franz Ferdinand of Austria and his wife were shot by Gavrilo Princip, a young Serbian nationalist committed to liberating Bosnia from the Austro-Hungarian yoke. The assassination in Sarajevo was not just a diplomatic crisis, but one of the triggers for a series of political and military events that would plunge Europe, and by extension the world, into the First World War.

In 1915, as the world conflict drew to a close, Pierre de Coubertin, who had become President of the IOC, took two major decisions to ensure the continued existence of the Olympic movement. Firstly, he moved the IOC headquarters to Lausanne, Switzerland, choosing this land of peace to preserve the organization's political neutrality in war-torn Europe. Secondly, he decided to maintain the name of "6th Olympiad" for the 1916 Games in Berlin, awarded in 1912, whether or not they actually took place. This move was intended to guarantee the continuity and legitimacy of the Olympic Games, despite the absence of a physical edition[12].

In the end, the 1916 Games were cancelled, as it was impossible to organize such an event in a Europe at war. The IOC's decision also took into account the unsuitability of such an event for the realities of the conflict, in particular the violation of Belgian neutrality by Imperial Germany. At the same time, Belgium, praised for its resistance to German occupation, offered to host the 1920 Games in Antwerp, circumstances permitting. This offer was strengthened when the city of Lyon, a candidate for 1920, agreed to support Antwerp and postpone its own bid until 1924, on condition that the Belgian city was liberated in time.

At the end of the war in 1918, Pierre de Coubertin entered into discussions with the Belgian Olympic Committee to turn this vision into reality. Convinced that Antwerp could symbolize the rebirth of Olympism and help rebuild Belgium after the trauma of the Great War, he obtained the necessary support. On April 5, 1919, Antwerp was officially awarded the title of host city for the 1920 Games,

---

12. BONIFACE Pascal, *JO politiques*, Éditions Eyrolles, 2016.

posing the daunting challenge of preparing a war-torn city in just sixteen months. The Belgian government made a financial commitment, covering half the costs of the Olympic facilities, underlining the political and symbolic importance of the Games as a message of peace and reconciliation.

The Political Exclusion of the "Defeated" of the Great War

In this post-war context, the IOC faced a complex dilemma. The 1919 Treaty of Versailles had redrawn the European map, punishing the defeated countries with heavy reparations and lost territories. How to maintain the universality and neutrality of the Olympic Games, while maneuvering with the political realities and prevailing sentiments among the victorious nations? Inviting the defeated countries could be perceived, by the victors of the war, as a provocation or a minimization of the suffering endured during this major conflict. Especially since the Games are being held in Belgium, which paid a heavy price during the conflict. The Allies had already taken the lead by organizing the Inter-Allied Games in July 1919 at the Pershing stadium in Paris, as a celebration of military victory through sport.

In the end, the IOC decided not to invite the "defeated" countries to the Antwerp Games: Germany, Austria, Hungary, Bulgaria and the Ottoman Empire. With this decision, the IOC adopted a controversial stance, since in wanting to preserve the Games' continuity, it took a political decision that went against the grain of the "neutrality" sought by the Charter at the time of the revival of Olympism. The example of the exclusion of certain countries from the 1920 Olympic Games reveals how the consequences of an international political situation—in this case, the aftermath and sanctions of the First World War—can have an influence on the Games, which are above all an arena for the representation of different national forces. The IOC's decision can thus be seen as a reflection of sanctions, of the "diplomacy of resentment" towards defeated countries, which consists in punishing them and excluding them from international relations.

Added to these political considerations was the position of the Soviet Empire, freshly established by the Bolshevik revolution of 1917. By refusing to take part in what they saw as a representation of capitalism and "petty bourgeois" games, the Soviets underlined another facet of the political complexity surrounding the organization of the 1920 Olympiad. Their absence not only marks an ideological divergence from the values promoted by Olympism at the time, but also underlines the emergence of new geopolitical cleavages that would shape the 20th century. The 1920 Games in Antwerp took place against a backdrop in which the Olympic movement's ambitions for neutrality and universality were put to the test by the political and ideological realities of the post-First World War world.

Antwerp 1920: The Symbol of Olympic Universalism

The Antwerp Olympics, with the participation of 29 nations and 2,626 athletes (including only 65 women), set a new record for international participation. Nations such as Brazil, Estonia, New Zealand, Czechoslovakia and Monaco made their first appearance. The Games also introduced two major innovations: the Olympic flag and the Olympic oath, reinforcing the idea of "world brotherhood" over and above political differences.

The Olympic flag, first introduced in 1913 by Pierre de Coubertin, consists of five interlaced rings on a white background. Each ring represents one of the world's five continents: Europe, Asia, Africa, America and Oceania. Their interlacing symbolizes the union and friendship between the peoples of these continents through sport, affirming the Olympic commitment to universality. The colors of the rings—blue, yellow, black, green and red—and the white background were selected for their presence on every national flag at the time, ensuring a symbolic representation of all the countries of the world. Coubertin himself emphasized the importance of this symbol: "Thus designed, it is symbolic; it represents the five parts of the world united by Olympism, and its six colors reproduce those of all the flags flying throughout the universe today."[13] For the first time, this flag flies at the Antwerp Games, visually embodying the spirit of unity that defines Olympism.

The Olympic oath, sworn by an athlete on behalf of all competitors, reinforces this notion of commitment to fair play and neutrality. With this oath, athletes undertake to respect and honor the rules of competition, symbolizing their dedication to the spirit of sportsmanship and ethics of the Olympic movement. The oath has evolved over the years to keep pace with modern developments, notably the fight against doping.

This Belgian Olympiad celebrates the USA, who dominate the medal table with an impressive total of 95 medals, including 41 golds, followed by Sweden (64) and Great Britain (43). This

---

13. WAWRZYNIAK Richard, *Histoire(s) des Jeux olympiques*, Mareuil Éditions, 2021.

remarkable American performance reflects not only their sporting excellence, but also the country's emergence as a post-war world power. Belgium won only 6 medals, but did manage to win gold in one of the most popular competitions of the Games: the Olympic soccer tournament[14].

Ultimately, the Antwerp Games confronted the Olympic movement with a dilemma: that of preserving the Games as a "universal and neutral" sporting event, while at the same time the Games remain a legacy of the Western powers, becoming an instrument of power for states and a platform for the assertion of their national identity, in an increasingly fraught geopolitical context. Lastly, they serve to highlight a country's ability to organize in the eyes of the world, reinforcing the competition to organize them, and even instrumentalizing them in the service of the host country's interests.

14. For more details, see my previous book, *Football Club Geopolitics. Mondial : 22 histoires insolites sur la Coupe du monde de football*, Max Milo, 2022.

Chapter 4 - 1936 Berlin: Using the Olympic Games to Further Nazi Ideology

The Berlin Games of 1936 go down in history as the emblem of the political instrumentalization of sport, exploited in the service of one of the darkest of causes: that of Hitler and Nazism. However, the genesis of the Games began in a radically different context, with the IOC vote on April 26, 1931 in Barcelona. Following the successful editions in Paris in 1924 and Amsterdam in 1928, no fewer than 14 cities expressed an interest in hosting the 1936 Olympic Games (Alexandria, Barcelona, Berlin, Budapest, Buenos Aires, Cologne, Dublin, Frankfurt, Helsinki, Lausanne, Montevideo, Nuremberg, Rio de Janeiro and Rome). However, the "Great Depression" of 1929 weakened the world economy, reducing the list to Barcelona and Berlin.

The Berlin dossier echoes the cancelled 1916 edition. It promised not only to rehabilitate a Germany that had been heavily punished by the Treaty of Versailles after the Great War, but also to use Olympism as a bridge towards reconciliation between formerly enemy nations. As for Barcelona's bid, a few days before the IOC vote, Spain entered a period of great political instability, with the recent proclamation of the Second Spanish Republic. These circumstances tipped the balance in Berlin's favor, offering Germany and the Weimar Republic an opportunity to rise again and re-enter the concert of nations.

However, the consequences of the economic crisis of 1929 did not spare Germany, exacerbating the tensions and economic difficulties inherited from the previous sanctions. In this climate of despair, extremist parties, led by Adolf Hitler's NSDAP, gained in popularity, promising to restore German order and grandeur. The political tide changed radically on January 30, 1933, when Hitler was swept to power at the ballot box, ushering in a dark era for the German nation, and for the Games themselves.

Ineffective Boycott Calls

The Berlin Olympics were not, at first, a priority for Hitler and the Nazi Party, who were reluctant to promote an event of international stature in the context of priority national projects. However, Joseph Goebbels, the Reich's Minister of Propaganda, quickly realized the potential of the Games as a powerful propaganda tool. He persuaded Hitler to seize the opportunity to promote the Nazi regime and its doctrine of Aryan supremacy, while portraying Germany as a world power, both respectable and peaceful in the eyes of the world. The budget increased from 2.6 million to 36 million Reichsmarks[15].

Nevertheless, the implementation of openly racist and anti-Semitic policies by the Nazi regime raised concerns within the IOC

---

15. THILOU Thomas, *Histoire(s) de Jeux : Les Jeux Olympiques de 1896 à 2021, 125 ans d'Humanité*, L'Harmattan, 2022.

and triggered an international reaction, leading to calls for a boycott from countries such as the UK, France, Sweden, Czechoslovakia, the Netherlands and the USA. The U.S. Olympic Association went so far as to suggest moving the 1936 Games to Rome. Faced with the threat to this 11th edition of the Olympic Games, Henri de Baillet-Latour, IOC President at the time, began tense negotiations on the possibility of keeping the Games in Berlin.

In response, the Nazi regime redoubled its efforts to reassure the international community and Olympic authorities. A carefully orchestrated visit by Baillet-Latour to Berlin in 1935, under strict surveillance, was organized. Officially, the regime pledged to organize a depoliticized event, open to Jewish athletes and other minorities, promising to respect the principles of the Olympic Charter and to allow the participation of "all races and confessions." In a conciliatory gesture towards the IOC, Hitler retained Theodor Lewald, perceived as a "half-Jew" by the Nazis, as President of the Organizing Committee.

These assurances seem to be enough to allay international fears. Calls for a boycott are less intense. The President of the U.S. Olympic Committee, Avery Brundage, asserts that "politics has no place in sport", and is also convinced by the Nazi authorities. The United States' decision to confirm its participation had a major impact, leading to a wave of commitments from other nations. Nevertheless, voices of protest continued to be heard. Spain, led by the Popular Front coalition of left-wing political forces, planned to organize a "People's Olympics" in Barcelona in July 1936, in opposition to Hitler's Games. The competition generated a great deal of enthusiasm, with almost 6,000 participants and dozens of national delegations planning to attend. Unfortunately, this wind of opposition was brutally interrupted by the nationalist military uprising of Franco's forces, leading to the cancellation of the Olympics and marking the start of the Spanish Civil War.

The Olympics, a Tool of Nazi Propaganda

The Nazi regime, under the firm grip of Adolf Hitler, mobilized all German resources for the spectacular staging of the Games. The aim was to usher the Games into a modern era, projecting an image of a powerful, "humanist" and peaceful Germany on the world stage, while promoting propaganda at home. Berlin 1936 was envisioned as a celebration of the Third Reich, through an unprecedented propaganda campaign. The Berlin Olympic Stadium, with its capacity of over 100,000 spectators, became the symbol of this demonstration of power. The media, under the aegis of the Goebbels Ministry of Propaganda, became the vectors for disseminating Nazi ideology, glorifying the superiority of the "Aryan race" and the virtues of strength and physical health. Leni Riefenstahl's film *Les Dieux du Stade* was the mainstay of this propaganda, transforming art into an instrument of power[16].

The introduction of television was a historic first, with the Games broadcast live on some twenty large screens installed across Berlin, providing unprecedented public immersion. This technological advance, coupled with the authorization given to broadcasting companies to retransmit the event to over 40 countries, amplified the reach of the Nazi propaganda machine. At the same time, the regime orchestrated visits for foreign journalists and dignitaries,

---

16. BROHM Jean-Marie, *1936 : Les Jeux olympiques à Berlin*, André Versaille éditeur, 2008.

offering them an idealized vision of Germany, while concealing the most repressive and inhumane aspects of the regime, such as the concentration camps and policies of racial exclusion.

Finally, the Nazi regime introduced a new feature to highlight its ideals and ensure that all of Germany and its people could be transcended by the Games: the Olympic torch relay. The flame had been reintroduced at the 1928 Olympic Games in Amsterdam, to revive this ancient tradition and keep this "sacred fire" burning throughout the Games' celebrations. Carl Diem, one of the members of the organizing committee, proposed going one step further: that the flame be transported from the birthplace of the Olympic Games, Olympia, to the host city, with a large parade leading up to the main stadium. The idea quickly won over Hitler, who endorsed the Olympic torch relay. A tradition that continues to this day.

Berlin 1936: Hitler and the Third Reich at the Center of the Arena

In the final preparations for the Games, the Nazi regime was faced with the need to maneuver between its discriminatory policies and the "universal" principles of Olympism. A façade was put in place to present relaxed segregation policies. Germany pledged not to exclude Jewish athletes from its delegation, although in reality, Hélène Mayer, the silver-winning German-Jewish fencer, was the only one to represent this pledge. This attempt to smooth out the Nazi image internationally was launched simultaneously with a "cleansing" campaign in Berlin, characterized by the removal of anti-Semitic signs, mass arrests and thousands of forced deportations. The marginal presence of minority athletes struggled to conceal internal persecution, highlighting the hypocrisy between the appearance of tolerance promoted by the regime and its repressive policies.

While Nazi Germany was being rebranded, the Berlin Games attracted a record 49 nations, surpassing the 37 of the previous edition. The Games saw the entry of new national delegations from around the world, including Afghanistan, Bermuda, Bolivia, Costa Rica and Liechtenstein. This European micro-state took part for the first time in a funny way. During the Games, Liechtenstein realized how similar its blue and red flag was to that of Haiti, so in 1937 a crown was added to its flag.

The opening ceremony was the apotheosis of this propaganda campaign. It opened with the impressive Hindenburg airship, with swastikas on all four rudders. Hitler's arrival at the podium, to the sound of Wagner's tribute march and Nazi salutes, ushered in a parade of nations: Greece in the lead, in keeping with Olympic tradition, and closing with the host country and its large delegation of athletes totally devoted to the Nazi regime. The Nazi salute of some athletes, in contrast to the various greetings of other delegations, illustrates the complexity of international reactions. Notably, the United States and the United Kingdom paid tribute without adopting the Nazi salute, demonstrating a form of resistance.

After a speech by the President of the German Olympic Committee, the Games were officially launched by Adolf Hitler: "I declare open the Olympic Games in Berlin, celebrating the eleventh Olympiad of the modern era."[17] This sober speech was part of a compromise reached by the IOC to ensure that Hitler did not

---

17. BOISSONADE Euloge, CHARPENTIER Henri, *La grande histoire des Jeux olympiques*, France Empire, 1999.

give the Games an overly propagandistic tone. Even if this was far from being the case during the events.

The Troublemaker Jesse Owens

However, one man was to upset the well-oiled machinery of Nazi propaganda: Jesse Owens. The black American athlete dazzled the Games with his talent, winning four gold medals (100 m, 200 m, long jump and 4×100 m relay). He undermined the Nazi ideology, which aimed to demonstrate the superiority of the "Aryan race" and impose a racist ideology. The notable interaction between Owens and Luz Long, his German rival, during the long jump event, illustrates a challenge to Nazi ideology through the very act of sporting fraternity. The images of Long sharing advice with Owens run counter to the racial doctrines promoted by the regime. Owens' performances in Berlin, performed before the eyes of a Nazi regime intent on using the event for propaganda purposes, served as a powerful counter-narrative. Every Owens victory reiterated the principles of human equality, in direct contrast to the ideology of the superiority of the Aryan race advocated by the Nazi regime.

However, it's worth noting that, despite Owens' exploits, Nazi Germany managed to present the Games as a success, improving its international image and demonstrating German power. As if to echo its return to the forefront of the world stage, it was indeed Germany that won its Olympic Games, topping the medal table (101) ahead of the United States (56) and Italy (27). Adolf Hitler's triumph at the Berlin Games, and the absence of concerted international opposition to their organization, reflected a certain passivity in the face of the rise of Nazism. This was particularly illustrated two years later, in 1938, with the Munich Agreement, when the French and British surrendered Czechoslovakia to Hitler in order to avert another large-scale conflict. An ominous prelude to the expansionism of the Third Reich, which a few years later would lead the world into a new world war.

CHAPTER 5 - 1940 TOKYO - HELSINKI: THE IMPOSSIBLE GAMES

The Berlin Games had not yet begun, but that year the IOC voted in favor of a controversial new host country for the 1940 edition: Japan, with the city of Tokyo. Japan's bid for the Olympic Games was no accident. As in the case of Germany, it reflects the political will to assert Japan as a rising and appeased power through the organization of such an event. Indeed, since the beginning of the 20th century, the Empire of the Rising Sun has been seeking to assert itself as a real power, notably through increasing expansionism and militarization.

This policy was delayed from the 1920s onwards, as Japan suffered several earthquakes, including the one in 1923 that killed over 100,000 people on the main island of Honshū. Japan managed to rebuild itself with renewed economic stability from the 1930s onwards, and continued its expansion in Asia by invading the Chinese territory of Manchuria in 1931. This occupation was immediately condemned by the international community, but Japan persisted, establishing the puppet state of Manchukuo in 1932. In the face of worldwide disapproval and condemnation of its actions by the UN's forerunner, the League of Nations (League), Japan chose to leave the organization in 1933.

The Olympic Games to Rehabilitate Japan's Image

Japan's bid for the 1940 Games was therefore designed to pursue a political strategy, that of installing Japan at the table of the world's greats, and the organization of an Olympiad could enable it to reinforce this credibility. The Olympics had become a modern event, and its organization by the host country sent a message to other countries, demonstrating its cultural and technological power, while promoting a message of peace behind the "universal" character of Olympism. The year 1940 is also a highly symbolic Japanese date, as it corresponds to Kigen-sestu, the 2,600th anniversary of the enthronement of Jinmu, the mythical founder of Japan, which can only reinforce patriotism in the country.

The campaign to choose the host city for the 1940 Olympics is, once again, intense, with not only Tokyo but also Barcelona, Rome and Helsinki in the running. The Olympic Games had established themselves as a major international event, and the competition for the right to host the Games was fierce. Japan's condemnation by the League of Nations did not prevent the IOC from choosing Tokyo's bid at its Berlin session on July 29 1936, by 37 votes to Helsinki's 26. The opportunity was too good for the Olympic organization to extend the Games to the Asian continent for the first time, marking the growing internationalization of its competition, which was not limited to the United States and Europe.

Tokyo 1940: An Edition Cancelled at the Instigation of the Japanese Empire's Expansionism

The IOC is once again faced with a dilemma. How do you promote an international event, which brings together more and more nations and is therefore charged with a geopolitical context, while maintaining a neutral political line? The debate was made all the more pressing by the fact that Tokyo's designation as host city for the 1940 Games followed on from the Berlin controversy of 1936. In other words, choosing to award the Games to countries run by authoritarian and aggressive governments, who will *de facto* use the event to legitimize their political regime and soften their country's image in the eyes of the world.

In the end, this debate never took place. As 1940 approached, Japan's aggressive policy on Chinese territory was put to the test. The conflict intensified in 1937 with the alliance between Mao Zedong's Chinese Communist forces and Chiang Kai-shek's Nationalists against Japanese forces, marking the start of the Second Sino-Japanese War. Voices were raised against holding the Games, arguing that national resources should be devoted entirely to the war effort. Japan tried to reassure the IOC at the Cairo session in 1937 that it would be able to organize the Games despite the conflict, but the situation within Japan was becoming increasingly tense. Finally, on July 15, 1938, the Japanese authorities took the decision to cancel the Games at a legislative session of the Imperial Diet. Kōichi Kido officially announced the cancellation the following day: "When peace reigns again in the Far East, we can invite the Games to Tokyo, and seize this opportunity to prove to the peoples of the world the true Japanese spirit". Kido, a key figure in Japanese politics in the 1945 surrender, didn't know it yet, but that moment wouldn't come until much later, in 1964, 26 years later.

Helsinki 1940: The Winter War Cancels the Games

All hell broke loose at the IOC. The outright cancellation of the 1940 event had to be avoided at all costs. New York, London, Rome and Helsinki took up positions, but it was the Finnish capital that quickly stood out. It had been the finalist bid against Tokyo, and Finland had offered to host the Games as early as March 1938, in the event of Japan's withdrawal. Finally, on September 3 of that year, at a meeting of the IOC Executive Committee in Brussels, the Games were officially awarded to Helsinki, and the event was scheduled to take place from July 20 to August 4, 1940. But the course of history was to decide otherwise.

Expansionist tendencies in the 1930s were not confined to Japan. In 1938, Germany annexed Austria, then the Sudetenland territories of Czechoslovakia, without any international reaction of condemnation. Germany's invasion of Poland on September 1, 1939, in accordance with a pact with the Soviet Union, prompted France and the United Kingdom to enter the war, and the outbreak of the Second World War. Finland was not to be spared, with pre-existing territorial tensions with its imposing Soviet neighbor, particularly over the strategic region of Karelia.

Karelia is a region divided between Finland and the USSR, and has historically been bitterly disputed between the two countries, particularly since Finland gained independence and broke away from Russian territory in 1917. Stalin took advantage of the inherent tensions in Europe to extinguish the pro-Finnish movement in Karelia and directly threaten Finland. He demanded that his neighbor cede significant border territories, citing the safety of Leningrad, just 32 km from the Finnish border. When Finland refused, Soviet power attacked Finnish territory on November 30, 1939. This marked the start of the "Winter War" and the scheduled end of the 1940 Games.

As Europe was plunged into war and the conflict globalized, Finland announced on April 21, 1940 that the Helsinki Games could not take place. Delaying the announcement as long as possible, IOC President Henri de Baillet-Latour of Belgium officially cancelled the 12th edition of the Games on May 2, 1940. The same decision was taken for the 1944 Games, which were awarded to London in June 1939, in the face of numerous other candidates (Rome, Detroit, Lausanne, Athens, Budapest, Helsinki and Montreal). Despite the cancellation of these Games, the IOC chose to consider these editions as an integral part of Olympic history, thus continuing Pierre de Coubertin's vision and placing Olympism in a historical continuity. The 1940 Games are therefore the 12th edition, and the 1944 Games the 13th, without actually having taken place.

The time of war plunged the world into horror until 1945. The Olympic flame was to shine again afterwards, in a bid to build a new world in search of peace. As witnessed by the creation of the United Nations Organization (UNO) at the San Francisco conference in 1945, with the signing of the Charter by some fifty states. London was chosen to take up the challenge of bringing nations together again in a spirit of brotherhood. This 1948 edition of the Games was, however, a reflection of the post-war consequences, and was renamed the "Austerity Games". They did, however, bring a surge of optimism to a rebuilding world, but the IOC and the

Olympic movement were soon confronted with a new global geopolitical context: the opposition between the two victorious superpowers of the war, the United States and its Western bloc versus the USSR and its Eastern bloc, which confirmed the beginnings of the Cold War.

Chapter 6 - 1952 Helsinki: From the "Cold War" to the "Medal War"

After the 1948 edition in London, limited and marked by the stigma of the Second World War, the 1952 edition in Helsinki marked the great return of the Olympic Games. However, the global configuration had changed considerably since 1939 and the cancelled 1940 Games, again scheduled to take place in Finland. The geopolitical landscape has undergone a radical metamorphosis, crystallizing around a bipolar opposition between the two great victors of the war: the USA and the USSR. This division accelerated between the two new superpowers, as a veritable bloc logic soon emerged. For Winston Churchill, Europe was now separated by an "iron curtain" of ideological and physical borders. The Western bloc, led by the powerful USA, brought together democratic, market-oriented nations, while the USSR's Eastern bloc brought together communist and socialist countries, characterized by centralized state control of the economy and society.

Although a new world war has recently ended, this rivalry does not prevent tensions that are already raising fears of a military response. The Berlin crisis of 1949, marked by the Soviet blockade of

West Berlin, symbolized this escalation of tensions. It led to the division of Germany into two: the Federal Republic of Germany (FRG), integrated into the Western bloc, and the German Democratic Republic (GDR), aligned with the USSR, thus extending the separation of Europe[18]. Each side set up a military alliance to prevent further conflict: NATO for the West in 1949, and the Warsaw Pact for the East in 1955. This period of geopolitical tension between the two blocs came to be known as the Cold War. There was no direct large-scale fighting between the two superpowers, but they each supported opposing sides in regional conflicts. The main proxy war illustrating this was the Korean War, which began in 1950 and pitted North Korea, supported by the USSR, against South Korea, backed by the USA and its allies.

The USSR's Opportunistic Entry into the Olympic Movement

Against this tense geopolitical backdrop, the 1952 Olympic Games promised to be a new battleground for the two rivals. On June 30, 1947, at the IOC Session in Stockholm, Helsinki was chosen as the host city ahead of Amsterdam, Athens, Stockholm and five American bids! The Finnish bid stood out thanks to a more solid proposal, benefiting from the infrastructures prepared for the cancelled 1940 edition. Although Helsinki was chosen for organizational reasons, this avoided many complications for the IOC and its desire to build a politically neutral "sporting world". Indeed, after the Second World War, Finland opted for a democratic regime while

---

18. We'll come back to this in more detail in chapter 9 on the two Germanies.

maintaining a neutral stance, in order to be in an intermediate zone between the Western and Eastern blocs. This strategy aimed to maintain trade with Western countries, while establishing ties with the USSR, its imposing neighbor, to avoid a repetition of the tensions that had led to the Winter War of 1939. With this in mind, Finland signed the YYA military treaty with the Soviet Union in 1948, a pact of friendship, cooperation and mutual assistance, thus consolidating its neutral position.

As Helsinki was not aligned with either sphere of influence, it was the moment chosen by the USSR in 1951 to ask the IOC for its integration into the Olympic movement and to attempt to participate in the Games for the first time. The USSR had long resisted the idea, even organizing its own Games with the Spartakiades[19] since the Olympics were seen as a reflection of capitalist ideology, but the Soviet powers seized the opportunity presented by the Finnish field to re-enter the Olympic arena. This strategic about-turn was not insignificant; it was part of a broader drive by the Soviet Union to promote its communist system and to measure itself, on a sporting and symbolic level, against its main rival, the United States.

The IOC accepted the application for membership, albeit with reservations about the amateur status of Soviet athletes. The latter were suspected of being hired by the army or the police, so that they could then train full-time, in contravention of the Olympic spirit and amateurism. Nonetheless, the Olympic organization seized the opportunity to transcend political divisions and make the Games a meeting point between two antagonistic blocs.

---

19. DUFRAISSE Sylvain, *Les héros du sport. Une histoire des champions soviétiques (années 1930-années 1980)*, Champ Vallon, 2019.

The Olympics, the New Battleground of the Cold War

However, the climate was not calmed: at the 1951 IOC Congress, the Soviet question was not the only thorny issue on the agenda. The IOC delegates also had to take into account other tense situations. Notably, the first participation of Israel (whose independence was contested by Arab countries following the Arab-Israeli war [1948-1949])[20], the division of Germany, and the repercussions of the Chinese civil war of 1949, which now saw "two Chinas" fighting each other.

Both the American and Soviet camps remained wary before the start of the Games. The USA's decision to participate was taken only after a careful assessment of the political situation in Finland. The USSR, for its part, initially planned to set up a daily shuttle service for its athletes between Leningrad and Helsinki, to avoid being on the same playing field as the Americans. However, thanks to Finnish diplomacy, the athletes from both camps will be reunited in Finland, but not in the same Olympic village. In fact, three separate villages were built, one for the men, one for the women and one for the Eastern bloc athletes, both men and women, isolated from the others in the Otaniemi village on the Baltic Sea.

This physical separation, far from being a simple logistical measure, shows the extent to which tensions are palpable in the run-up to the opening ceremony. The decision to isolate the athletes from the Eastern bloc did not come from the IOC, but from the USSR, heralding a long period of political manoeuvring by the Olympic organization to maintain the "universal" illusion of the Games.

---

20. We'll come back to this in more detail in Chapter 18, Israel-Palestine.

The Case of Germany and China

The IOC is not out of the woods yet, as geopolitical situations are having a direct impact on the Helsinki Games. First and foremost, the participation of Germany. Absent from the 1948 Games, the IOC was determined not to repeat the mistakes of the Antwerp Games and to reinstate the German delegation for the 1952 Games. This was achieved with the integration of the West German Olympic Committee into the Olympic movement in 1949. However, the IOC rejected the creation of an East German Olympic Committee, pointing out that one already existed in West Germany, and that the GDR was not recognized by the "international community" as a state. The problem was that Germany was now *de facto* divided into two distinct states. The Olympic movement tried to circumvent this de facto situation by reuniting the two Germanies under a single banner. The attempt failed, however, as the German delegation took part only with athletes from West Germany, the GDR having refused to unite under a common German team.

Another point of tension arises with China. The Communist victory in the Chinese Civil War of 1949 led to the founding of the People's Republic of China (PRC) by Mao Zedong. At the same time, Chiang Kai-shek's nationalists took refuge on the island of Taiwan, formerly under Japanese control, and saw themselves as the legitimate representatives of China. This division gave rise to the unique situation of two governments claiming the name "Republic of China", each with its own territorial claims and political vision for China's future. The Olympic ground is at the heart of this struggle, all the more so as the IOC is inviting both delegations. Four days after the start of the Helsinki Games, the "Republic of China" (Taiwan) withdrew its athletes in protest against the IOC's decision to allow athletes from the "People's Republic of China" to compete. The PRC hardly benefited from this, as only one athlete (swimmer Wu Chuanyu) from its 40-member delegation arrived in time to take part in the official competition. As we shall see later, the PRC would not return to the Olympics until the 1984 edition in Los Angeles.

Helsinki 1952: The Start of the "Medal War"

Despite these complications, the fact that the 1952 Games were held in Finland, a territory not involved in the struggle for influence between the two blocs, ensured record participation. Nearly 4,932 athletes (including just 521 women) from 69 countries took part in Helsinki. The Bahamas, the People's Republic of China, Guatemala, Hong Kong, Indonesia, Israel, the Netherlands Antilles, Nigeria, Thailand, Vietnam and, of course, the USSR took part in their first Olympics. Some countries not yet fully autonomous, but still in the process of decolonization, also took part in the Games. One example was the Gold Coast, still under British rule at the time, but whose participation under its own colors paved the way for the country's independence in 1957, when it became Ghana.

Whereas the United States had been in the lead at previous Games, the Helsinki Games saw a real battle for first place on the medal table. The final result shows how the Games became a new battleground for the two Cold War rivals: the USA dominated with 76 medals, including 40 gold, but the USSR made a stunning entry with 71 medals, including 22 gold, in its first participation. Finland, host of the Games, also stood out with 22 medals. The Games were marked above all by the remarkable performances of Soviet athletes: Viktor Chukarin, with four gold medals in gymnastics, and above all Emil Zátopek, who won the 5,000 m, 10,000 m and the prestigious marathon event. The USSR didn't hesitate to transform the results into a metaphor for the political success of its model, as the national sports daily *Sovetsky Sport* wrote during the Games: "Every record won by our athletes, every victory in international competitions clearly demonstrates to the whole world the advantages and strength of the Soviet system."

The Helsinki Olympics made the Olympics more than just a sporting event. They became a manifestation of the ideological struggle of the Cold War, where every medal was a symbolic victory over the opposing bloc. And Helsinki was only the first of many.

CHAPTER 7 - 1956 MELBOURNE: FROM THE SUEZ CRISIS TO THE "BLOODBATH"

The selection of Melbourne as host city for the 1956 Olympic Games, at the IOC Session in Rome on April 28, 1949, marked a historic moment for several reasons. The decision was significant not only because it awarded the Olympic Games to the Southern Hemisphere and Oceania for the first time, but also because it reflected the IOC's desire to broaden the geographical scope of the Olympic movement. As in 1952, the Games were to provide a forum for the many geopolitical contexts of the time. In addition to the Cold War, which dominated international debates, other tensions were added to an already fraught context. The Chinese case, already present at the 1952 Olympic Games, persisted as the IOC once again invited delegations from the "People's Republic of China" (PRC) and the "Republic of China" (Taiwan). It's a real ideological battle between the two entities to claim the legitimacy of the name "China" on the international stage. This time, Mao Zedong's PRC boycotted the Games.

The Suez Crisis Invites Itself to the Melbourne Games

Another key event politicized the 1956 Olympic Games, just a few weeks before the opening ceremony on November 22: the Suez crisis. In July 1956, Egyptian President Nasser nationalized the Suez Canal, a vital artery for international trade, and in particular for the transport of European oil, previously controlled by a Franco-British company. Egypt's decision was aimed at financing the Aswan dam project, but it also raised concerns among Western powers about access to the canal. In response, Israel (already in conflict with Egypt following the first Arab-Israeli war of 1948), followed by the former British and French colonial powers, launched a military operation on Egyptian soil on October 29, 1956. Officially, the aim was to regain control of the canal and secure navigation, but in reality it was an attempt to overthrow Nasser and re-establish Western influence in the region. The operation triggered an international crisis, with the American and Soviet superpowers joining in and opposing the invasion for strategic and political reasons. International pressure, particularly from the United States, which threatened economic sanctions, finally forced the coalition to withdraw.

Although Egypt won a highly symbolic victory in the context of decolonization, tensions were still palpable. Egypt informed the IOC that its national delegation would boycott the Games if Israel participated. The reason: Israeli troops have not yet withdrawn from the Sinai region of Egypt. Faced with the absence of an IOC decision, Egypt and some of its allies (Iraq, Lebanon and Cambodia) decided to boycott the Games.

The Background to the Budapest Uprising

Another significant political event was to have an impact on the course of the following Games. On October 23, 1956, the Hungarian Revolution began, a popular uprising against the government of the Hungarian People's Republic and its subordination to the Soviet Union. These acts of resistance marked the start of an armed struggle, leading to intense clashes and the formation of revolutionary militias. Imre Nagy, a reform-minded Communist politician and leader of the revolt, took over as head of government, promising reforms and announcing Hungary's withdrawal from the Warsaw Pact, the Eastern Bloc's military alliance. This attempted revolution in one of the "People's Democracies" was brutally suppressed by Soviet forces, with over a thousand tanks sent into the streets of Budapest. The crackdown ended on November 10, 1956, with 3,000 Hungarians killed, 13,000 injured and 200,000 forced into exile. In reaction to the Soviet invasion of Hungary, the Netherlands, Spain and Switzerland boycott the 1956 Olympic Games, in solidarity with the Hungarian people and to condemn Soviet aggression.

In response to these events, the IOC, now presided over by the American Avery Brundage, a fervent advocate of the apolitical nature of sport, was faced with the challenge of making eminently political decisions while preserving the neutrality enshrined in the Olympic Charter. Brundage insisted that the Games should not be used as a stage for political demonstrations or boycotts, and that the Olympics should transcend political conflicts. Despite these numerous international crises, only eight countries decided to boycott (Egypt, Iraq, Lebanon, Cambodia, Spain, Netherlands, Switzerland, PRC), but this was already a sign that the Olympics were increasingly perceived as an arena for political demands. The Melbourne

Games were also a success in terms of the participating nations. Significantly, athletes from East and West Germany competed under the same banner, forming the United German Team. 67 national delegations competed in total, with the first participations of independent nations, following the decolonization process, such as Ethiopia, Fiji, Kenya and Liberia.

We could even go further, with 72 participating nations, if we take into account one of the special features of these Games. The Games were held not only in Australia, but also in Sweden. Australia had adopted a very firm provision requiring all imported animals to remain in quarantine for a long period, to prevent the spread of disease. As a result, the equestrian competitions were held in Stockholm, Sweden, over 15,000 km from the Australian Olympic site and 5 months before the opening ceremony. As a result, some of the nations that boycotted the Games in November 1956 took part in certain events.

Melbourne's "Bloodbath"

Despite the fine message of peace embodied by the unified German delegation, these Australian Games were to be marked by the context of the Hungarian revolution and the manifestation of tensions between Hungary and the USSR. This began on November 23, during the 10,000-meter race. Soviet runner Vladimir Kuts won the gold medal, beating out Hungarian Josef Kovacs, who refused to congratulate his opponent during the awards ceremony.

But the most memorable episode, which made headlines around the world, was the heated water polo match between the Hungarian and Soviet teams, dubbed the "Melbourne Bloodbath".

On December 6, 1956, Hungary and the USSR battled it out for a place in the final of the men's water polo tournament. The Hungarian players, aware of the underlying political context, entered the match with a deliberate strategy to provoke their Soviet opponents. Ervin Zádor, one of the key players in this match, reveals that the intention was to "make the Russians angry to distract them", exploiting their knowledge of the Russian language learned at school.

From the outset, the encounter was marked by an unusual intensity, with punches and kicks raining down from both sides. One particularly significant moment is captured on video: Dezső Gyarmati, the Hungarian captain, throws a punch at his Soviet opponent. Meanwhile, Zádor, backed by the cheers of the crowd chanting "Hajrá Magyarok!" ("Go Hungarians!"), scores two goals, strengthening his team's lead. Tension reached a climax with a minute to go, Hungary leading 4-0. It was at this point that Ervin Zádor, after a verbal exchange with Valentin Prokopov, was struck in the face by the latter during a stoppage in play, causing a large cut which drew blood in the pool. The incident set off a chain reaction among the spectators, already electrified by the match. The situation quickly degenerated, forcing the police to intervene to prevent a riot. The images of Zádor's injury, broadcast worldwide, crystallize the match as a "bloodbath", although Zádor himself later refutes reports of a blood-red pool. The referees decide to stop the match, declaring Hungary the winner. The hero of the match declared afterwards: "We felt we were playing not only for ourselves, but for our whole country"[21].

---

21. ABRAMS Roger I., *Playing Tough: The World of Sports and Politics*, UPNE, 2013.

This semi-final victory led to Hungary's final match against Yugoslavia. The Hungarian team triumphed once again, winning its fourth Olympic gold medal in water polo and giving a whole nation a chance to shine after the terrible events of the Hungarian revolution a few weeks earlier. Zádor and many of his team-mates did not have time to celebrate this title at home. Like many of their compatriots, they fled to the West, seeking to escape the sanctions imposed by the Soviet regime. Of the 112 members of the Hungarian delegation, only 44 returned to Budapest.

USSR Topples USA in the Medals Table

Following on from the Hungarian athletes' symbolic act of resistance, the Games also highlighted the Soviet Union's growing power on the international sporting stage. With 98 medals, including 37 gold, for the USSR, compared with 74 medals, including 32 gold, for the USA, the results in Melbourne reflected Soviet ambitions in their quest for superiority over their American rivals. This Soviet Olympic success was historic, as it was the first time since 1936 that the United States had not dominated the medal table.

It is also the opposition of two political models through sport. The American model is liberal, favoring private investment and individual sporting success, thanks in particular to a high-performance university system with little state intervention. The Soviet model, on the other hand, is interventionist, with sport governed by political authority and a focus on mass sport[22]. A *Pravda* journalist summed

---

22. GYGAX Jérôme, *Olympisme et guerre froide culturelle. Le prix de la victoire américaine*, L'Harmattan, 2012.

up the sporting victories of the Soviets and their allies as "dazzling proof that socialism is the system best suited to man's physical and spiritual fulfillment". This sporting and ideological battle illustrates the beginnings of an intense rivalry between the two superpowers in many fields, notably marked by the conquest of space and the first Soviet victories embodied by Sputnik and Yuri Gagarin.

In the final analysis, this second USSR vs. USA Olympics testifies to a dynamic of rivalry and competition that characterized the Cold War, and which was to take on a new dimension on the sporting stage. These Games not only reflected the political and ideological tensions of the time, but also highlighted the superpowers' desire to project their influence and assert their superiority far beyond the traditional boundaries of military and political confrontation. The editions in Moscow in 1980 and Los Angeles in 1984 culminated in a boycott that became the new instrument of opposition between the two blocs.

Chapter 8 - 1968 Mexico: Beyond the Raised Fists

At the turn of 1968, the world found itself at a political cross-roads, marked by the culmination of Cold War tensions and social protest on an unprecedented scale in various countries. The year became the symbol of a global struggle for civil rights, social justice and freedom (illustrated in particular in France with the events of May 1968), representing the aspirations and tensions of an era in turmoil. Against this backdrop, the Olympic Games in Mexico City came to be seen as a reflection of international negotiations, a platform for a number of new nations, as well as for societal demands.

With the process of decolonization and the UN's affirmation of the "right of peoples and nations to self-determination", new states emerged, seeking to legitimize their existence on the international stage. Sports recognition, notably by the IOC, which validates the membership of National Olympic Committees (NOCs) in the Olympic movement, also becomes a symbol of their sovereignty, attesting to their status as independent states in the eyes of the world. This was illustrated by a steady increase in the number of participating countries: 67 at the Melbourne Olympics in 1956, 83 in Rome in 1960, 93 in Tokyo in 1964, and soon over 112 national delegations for the Mexico Games.

A Context of Demands from Both Sides of the Blocks

The IOC broke new ground by voting to award the 1968 Games to a country like Mexico. For the first time, the Olympic movement chose a bid from an emerging "Third World" power, reflecting not only the expansion of the Olympic movement, but also the global dynamic of the non-aligned movement, eager to free itself from the polarities of the Cold War. The IOC then sought to build its own path, to free itself from the logics of blocs and to internationalize its Olympics even further. In choosing Mexico City, the IOC seized the opportunity to diversify geographically the hosting of the Olympic Games, until then mainly organized by Western countries, thus extending the reach of the Olympic movement beyond its traditional borders.

The 1968 Games took place against a tumultuous global backdrop, marked by numerous social protest movements that shook the various Cold War blocs. In the United States, the fight for civil rights, led by emblematic figures such as the Reverend Martin Luther King, aimed to dismantle the foundations of racial segregation and achieve equality for African-Americans. Luther King's assassination on April 4, 1968 sent shockwaves through the nation, exacerbating racial tensions and heightening the call for immediate social reform. At the same time, American military involvement in Vietnam provoked growing protest, giving rise to a vigorous movement advocating peace and openly criticizing American military interventionism. The Eastern bloc and Soviet hegemony were also called into question, particularly in Europe with the Prague Spring. Reform initiatives in Czechoslovakia, aimed at introducing "socialism with a human face", were violently halted by the intervention of Warsaw Pact forces in August 1968. This shock marked not only the failure of an attempt at liberalization, but also the beginning of a broader awareness of the oppression exercised by the USSR over its "satellite states".

10 Days before the Games: the Tlatelolco Massacre

Mexico was not exempt from these social tensions. Under the leadership of the Partido Revolucionario Institucional (PRI) and its authoritarian leader, Gustavo Díaz Ordaz, the country went through a period of growing protest throughout the 1960s. Demonstrations multiplied, demanding a fairer distribution of wealth and greater investment in health and education. Although the central government had so far succeeded in suppressing these uprisings by force, it was faced with a crisis of unprecedented proportions in the run-up to the Olympic Games, to be held on its soil in October. In August 1968, almost 300,000 people took to the streets of the capital to protest.

The unthinkable happened on October 2, 1968, 10 days before the opening of the Games: the Tlatelolco massacre. Thousands of students gathered in the Plaza de los Tres Culturas, in Mexico City's Tlatelolco district, shouting *"No queremos olimpiadas, queremos revolución!"* ("We don't want the Olympic Games, we want revolution!") On the orders of President Gustavo Díaz Ordaz, the army brutally intervened, opening fire on an unarmed crowd. The bloody crackdown left around 400 people dead and over 1,000 wounded.

Claude Kiejman, *Le Monde*'s Mexico City correspondent, described the horror on the spot: "It's the first time in my long career that I've seen soldiers fire on a cornered, defenseless crowd"[23].

Despite the scale of this bloody repression, official reactions from foreign governments were relatively restrained. The IOC turned a deaf ear. Its president, Avery Brundage, a fervent supporter of a strict separation between sport and politics, made no statement. For him, sport must be disconnected from politics and "domestic politics". Despite the scale of the tragedy, sport must go on, whatever the political and social realities of the host country. The silence of the IOC and the lack of any immediate questioning of the Games underline an era when the separation between these spheres was considered paramount, sometimes to the detriment of justice and human dignity.

Mexico 1968: When the Olympic Games Became the Athletes' Political Forum

However, the 1968 Olympic Games were even more political than previous editions: this time, the athletes used the Olympic stage as a platform for their demands. For example, the repression associated with the Prague Spring was echoed all the way to Mexico City. During the medal ceremony for the beam event, Natalia Kuchinskaya of the Soviet Union won gold in a controversial competition. Czechoslovak gymnast Věra Čáslavská, already voted her country's Sportswoman of the Year 4 times, dissented. In a discreet but powerful manner, she bows her head and looks

---

23. Boniface Pascal, *JO politiques*, Éditions Eyrolles, 2016.

away during the Soviet national anthem, a protest she will repeat on the podium alongside Soviet Larisa Petrik. In response, the Czechoslovak regime, now under the total control of the USSR, severely punished her, banning her from competitions and international travel for many years, reducing her to the status of a pariah until the fall of communism in Czechoslovakia[24].

Another gesture, at a medal ceremony, was to make even more news and go down in history. On October 16, 1968, in Mexico City, Tommie Smith and John Carlos, gold and bronze medallists respectively in the 200-metre event, were on the podium for the medal ceremony. To the sound of the American national anthem *The Star-Spangled Banner*, the two athletes raised a black-gloved fist. A powerful gesture symbolizing the fight for civil rights and solidarity with all those who suffer racial injustice in the USA and elsewhere. Their action was a deliberate expression of protest against racial discrimination, inspired by the Black Power movement, seeking to draw international attention to racial inequality and violence in their country. Alongside them, Australian silver medallist Peter Norman showed his support by wearing an Olympic Human Rights Project badge, underlining unity in the fight for equality and justice across racial and national boundaries. Smith would later declare, "If I win, I'm an American, not a black American. But if I did something wrong, then they'd say I'm a black man. We are black and we are proud to be black. Black America will understand what we did tonight."[25]

With this gesture, the three protagonists put the issue of civil rights and racial segregation at the center of the media

---

24. Radio Prague International, "V ra áslavská was born 80 years ago", May 1, 2022.
25. "1968: Black athletes make silent protest", BBC.com, October 17, 1968.

platform provided by the Olympic Games. The IOC, for its part, was red-faced, as the athletes were politicizing the Games and thus violating the Olympic Charter. Avery Brundage reacted swiftly, considering the action inappropriate for the neutral space that the Games should represent. Brundage ordered the immediate suspension of Smith and Carlos from the US team and their expulsion from the Olympic Village. Faced with resistance from the U.S. Olympic Committee, he threatens to disqualify the entire U.S. track and field team, which ultimately leads to the expulsion of the two athletes. The American press also criticized the athletes' attitude. *Time* magazine, on October 25, 1968, summed up the incident in stark contrast to Olympic ideals: "'Faster, higher, stronger' is the motto of the Olympic Games. 'Angrier, meaner, uglier' better describes the scene in Mexico City last week."[26] Peter Norman would also suffer the consequences of his solidarity, as he was sanctioned by the Australian delegation, not selected for the 1972 Olympics despite his qualifying performances, and even not invited to the Sydney Olympics in 2000. Despite the sanctions against Smith and Carlos, American athletes Lee Evans, Larry James and Ronald Freeman, who achieved a hat-trick in the 400 meters, also denounced racial segregation by taking to the podium wearing a black beret.

Like a symbol, the Mexico Olympics also highlighted former territories that had been victims of racial segregation, notably the newly independent African countries and the first participation of Central Africa, Congo-Kinshasa (formerly the Democratic Republic of Congo), Guinea and Sierra Leone. African athletes won at least one medal in all the running events, including Kenya's

---

26. "The *TIME* Vault: October 25, 1968", TIME.com.

impressive haul of 9 medals, including 3 golds, placing 14th out of 112 national delegations.

Despite the IOC's firm response and the attacks on Smith and Carlos, Mexico City marks a turning point in terms of the politicization of a sporting event. The Olympic Games are not just a space for nations to express themselves, but also a place where athletes can, and must, express their positions on universal societal issues, despite the fact that they are the main players in the Olympic arena.

Chapter 9 - 1972 Munich: The Paradox of the Two Germanys

In 1972, four years after the Mexico Games, the new Olympiad was held in Munich, Germany. This edition of the Games was distinguished by a notable peculiarity: it saw the participation of two German delegations under completely different flags and anthems. Although Germany has been divided into two distinct states (FRG and GDR) since 1949, this was a first at Olympic level. A paradoxical situation at a time when, at the dawn of the 1970s, the two Germanies were engaged in a historic diplomatic rapprochement, but when the Games would ultimately become a new arena for rivalries to demonstrate the superiority of one model over the other.

The Origins of the "Two Germanys"

After the fall of the Nazi regime in 1945, Germany was left in ruins and divided into four zones of occupation: American, British, French and Soviet, with Berlin, its capital, also split into four. This division took place at a time of growing tension between the USA and the USSR, marking the start of the Cold War. The merging of the three Western zones into one irritated the USSR and led to the Berlin crisis. This led to the establishment of two German states in 1949: the Federal Republic of Germany (FRG) in the West, aligned with the Western bloc of the USA, and the German Democratic Republic (GDR) in the East, under Soviet influence. To rebuild themselves and regain their prestige on the international stage after the war, the FRG and the GDR saw sport as a means of legitimization, distinction and rediscovered national pride. Soccer offered West Germany its first opportunity to shine, thanks to the "Miracle of Bern"[27], when its national team unexpectedly won the World Cup in 1954, sparking scenes of jubilation and joy throughout Germany, including the GDR.

In the Olympic field, East-West tensions had repercussions on the German sports organization. The IOC initially rejected the creation of an East German Olympic Committee, pointing out that one already existed in West Germany, and that the GDR was not universally recognized as a state. Of course, the IOC wanted to maintain political neutrality, but it was still an organization from the Western world. Recognizing the East German Olympic Committee at a time when the Western bloc did not recognize the GDR could also have had a political connotation, being seen as the first step towards legitimizing and potentially "validating" the communist model.

---

27. For more details, see my previous book, *Football Club Geopolitics. Mondial: 22 histoires insolites sur la Coupe du monde de football*, Max Milo, 2022.

German Olympic "Unity" in the Face of the Berlin Wall

In an attempt to transcend political divisions through sport, the IOC initiated a bold plan to unite East and West German athletes in a single team for the Olympic Games. Faced with growing isolation and limited international recognition, the GDR reluctantly agreed to join forces with its Western counterpart. Although reluctantly taken, this decision was preferred to non-participation, which would inevitably have benefited West Germany. Avery Brundage, the American President of the IOC and a fervent advocate of apolitical sport, sees the union as a symbolic success: "We have achieved in sport what politicians have failed to achieve up to now". As a token of unity, the two Germanies set aside their national anthems during ceremonies in favor of Beethoven's *Ode to Joy*. This sporting entente, embodied by the Unified German Team, continued for the 1960 and 1964 Games, when athletes competed under the name "Germany", under a specific Olympic flag: a black, red and yellow German flag incorporating the white Olympic rings.

However, the differences between the two German states gradually became more pronounced, with each striving to promote the superiority of its own political system, while at the same time becoming more entrenched in the alliances of opposing blocs. In 1955, the FRG joined NATO, while the GDR joined the Warsaw Pact, thus consolidating the "Iron Curtain" dividing Eastern and Western Europe. This competition between political models was also reflected at home, with demonstrations in the GDR and economic challenges leading to significant emigration. Between 1949 and 1961, almost 3 million East Germans used the Berlin Gateway to escape political repression and economic stagnation in the GDR. To stem this exodus, the East German government, with the support of the USSR, erected the Berlin Wall on the night of August 12-13, 1961. The wall became the symbol of the division of Germany, embodying the ideological, political and physical separation of the country and becoming an emblem of the Cold War.

Faced with the political reality of two Germanies operating under divergent political and ideological systems, the IOC had to adapt and go beyond its neutrality. Logistical challenges, such as the travel restrictions imposed on athletes between East and West, exacerbated the need for the GDR to assert its independent participation in the Olympic Games under its own banner. This aspiration became all the more pressing when, for the 1964 Games, a greater number of East German athletes qualified than their Western counterparts, underlining the GDR's sporting emergence on the international stage.

In 1965, the IOC granted the GDR the right to be represented by a separate National Olympic Committee, marking the official end of the Unified German Team. This development became a reality at the 1968 Winter Olympics in Grenoble and the Summer Olympics in Mexico City, where, for the first time, athletes from both delegations marched separately, although a common Olympic flag continued to fly. The IOC's recognition of two separate national entities reflected the acceptance of an inescapable geopolitical reality: Germany, as the scene of East-West confrontation, embodied the deep division that ran through the world during the Cold War. In adapting to this new situation, the IOC implicitly recognized the complexity of maintaining political neutrality in a context marked by pronounced ideological and territorial divisions.

Munich 1972: Ostpolitik *vs.* State Plan 14.25

A paradoxical situation, as we mentioned at the start of this chapter, since it was indeed West Germany, through the city of Munich, that was chosen in 1965 to host the 1972 Games. A paradox, since at the end of the 1960s, West German Chancellor Willy Brandt initiated a rapprochement with the GDR with his *Ostpolitik*. At the heart of this diplomatic initiative lay the conviction that dialogue and engagement could lead to a reduction in tensions and peaceful coexistence, even in the midst of deep ideological division.

This policy of détente in diplomatic relations between the two Germanies even led to the fundamental treaty of 1972, which led to mutual recognition between the two states, paving the way for their admission to the UN the following year, in 1973. The Munich Games could have been the forum to embody this diplomatic détente. All the more so as these Games aspired to turn the page on Germany's Nazi past and the 1936 Berlin Olympics, with the ambition of presenting a peaceful and welcoming Germany, as underlined by the motto *"Die Heiteren Spiele"* (*The Joyful Games*). Nevertheless, the split had already taken place, and the Games even anchored this sporting division, with both teams using their own flag and national anthem for the first time, burying German Olympic unity for good.

It's hard to imagine such a rapprochement between the two Germanies at these Games, since the GDR had found in sport a means of asserting its ideological and political superiority over the FRG. The East German regime was ready for anything, setting up a system of state-sponsored doping in the 1960s to dominate sporting competitions and win as many medals as possible as proof of the superiority of its socialist model. This doping system was introduced as a genuine planning policy, codenamed "State Plan

14.25". It involved the systematic doping of athletes, often without their knowledge, with anabolic substances designed to significantly improve their physical performance. Estimates suggest that up to 10,000 athletes were subjected to these practices in the two decades following the introduction of the program, with devastating consequences for their health[28].

The East German delegation won its first battle at the 1968 Olympic Games in Mexico City, finishing 5th on the medal table, while its West German rival finished 8th. The situation was even more glaring at the end of the Munich Games, with the GDR on the podium (3rd), behind the untouchable USSR and USA, with 66 medals won, while the FRG took just 40. This East German feat, though remarkable, remains overshadowed in the collective memory by a tragic event that left a profound mark on Olympic history.

Munich 1972: The Painful Context of the Israeli-Palestinian Conflict

The tragic episode at the Munich Olympics remains one of the darkest pages in the history of the Games. On September 5, a terrorist group affiliated to the Palestine Liberation Organization (PLO), known as Black September, broke into the Olympic Village and took eleven members of the Israeli delegation hostage. The hostage-taking resulted in the deaths of eleven Israeli athletes and coaches, as well as a West German policeman. This tragedy took place in a geopolitical context marked by growing tensions in the Middle East and the persistence of Israeli-Arab conflicts. Since the

28. THOMAZEAU François, *Histoire secrète du sport*, La Découverte, 2019.

creation of the State of Israel in 1948, tensions between Israel and its Arab neighbors have steadily escalated, culminating in several open wars, including the 1948 war, the 1956 Suez Canal crisis and the 1967 Six-Day War[29].

The latter, in particular, had far-reaching repercussions, leading to Israel's occupation of significant territories, including the West Bank, Gaza and the Golan Heights, exacerbating Palestinian national claims and fuelling resentment in the Arab world. Through this terrorist act, Black September sought to draw international attention to the Palestinian cause, exploiting the global visibility of the Olympic Games. In the wake of this tragedy, the IOC takes the controversial decision to continue the Games after a short period of mourning, once again crystallizing a debate on the place of politics and geopolitical conflicts in the supposedly neutral and peaceful Olympic framework.

German Reunification through Sport

The separation of the German Olympic teams had a particular resonance, underlining the tangible division between the two Germanies. As historians Kay Schiller and Christopher Young note, "perhaps more than any other sector of public life, Olympic sport confronted its officials with the stark reality of German division"[30]. This reality crystallized not only in the separation of teams, but also in the differences in approach to training and preparation, notably

---

29. We'll come back to this event in more detail in chapter 18 on the Israeli-Palestinian conflict, particularly in the context of Paris 2024.
30. BLAKEMORE Erin, "A Divided Germany Came Together for the Olympics Decades Before Korea Did", History.com, February 12, 2018.

with the state doping program launched by East Germany in the 1970s. Although long suspected, this program was not fully revealed until 1993, after the dissolution of the GDR, but it enabled the East German regime to use the many medals won by its athletes to promote its political regime and distinguish itself from its neighbor to the West.

From then on, the countries were irrevocably separated on the Olympic field, and political boycotts further separated the two teams at the Olympic Games in the years that followed. The fall of the Berlin Wall on November 9, 1989 marked the start of a new era for Germany. This reunification was consolidated on the sporting field, illustrated by the victory of the unified German national team at the 1990 Football World Cup, and by an Olympic delegation finally united at the 1992 Barcelona Olympics.

Chapter 10 - 1976 Montreal:
Apartheid: The First Major Boycott of the Olympic Games

From the 1950s onwards, the process of decolonization within the former empires and the bipolarization of the world between the Eastern bloc and the Western bloc prompted the newly independent countries to create a "third way", away from the tensions of the Cold War and neo-imperialism. This "non-aligned" movement took concrete form at the Bandung conference in Indonesia in 1955, with Zhou Enlai's China, Tito's Yugoslavia, Nehru's India and Nasser's Egypt leading the way. The war in Vietnam, led by the United States, and the growing influence of the USSR in the internal affairs of young independent countries reinforced this movement and the desire for autonomy in the face of superpower logic.

It was against this backdrop that the vote to choose the host city for the 1976 Olympic Games took place. At the IOC session on May 12, 1970, Los Angeles, Moscow and Montreal were still in the running. The United States and the USSR made considerable efforts to secure the organization of this international sporting extravaganza. However, to everyone's surprise, it was the Canadian city that won the bid, on the strength of its successful experience with the 1967 World's Fair. In fact, this vote came as little more than a half-surprise, as the IOC members were demonstrating their desire to universalize the Olympic Games, to take this flagship event beyond the logic of the East/West blocs, and not to be a mere adjustment variable.

Olympism in the Face of Apartheid

As we saw in 1968, the Olympics became a platform for conveying a message against segregationist and racist policies. While the case of the Mexico Games, through the raised fists of Tommy Smith and John Carlos, highlighted the situation in the United States, subsequent editions were marked by the situations in Rhodesia (now Zimbabwe) and South Africa. The South African case will come under particular scrutiny because of the *apartheid* system.

This policy of racial segregation was gradually put in place with the arrival in power in 1948 of the National Party: the political force that brought together the white Afrikaner and English-speaking populations, in a South African state that had already been heavily impacted by segregation at the beginning of its history in the 20th century. The establishment of apartheid can hardly be explained by the historical anxiety of the Afrikaners. This white ethnic community, descended from the first Dutch, French, German and Scandinavian settlers to reach South African territory, was obsessed by the fear of being "swallowed up" by the indigenous black peoples (who represented nearly 80% of the South African population at the beginning of the 20th century). This irrational fear led to a severe regime of racial segregation, with a system of social stratification:

white citizens had the highest status, followed in descending order by Asians, blacks and black Africans. National sports delegations were also affected, with a strict separation between white and "colored" teams[31]. This policy gradually isolated the South African state from the African and international scene. South Africa was excluded from the Commonwealth in 1961, and an arms embargo was voted by the United Nations Security Council in 1963. Faced with protests from several national Olympic committees and threats of boycott, particularly from Africa, the IOC was forced to take action by excluding the South African delegation from the 1964 Tokyo Olympic Games, where "racial non-mixity" was imposed, and then on a permanent basis from 1970 onwards.

This dynamic was broadened in 1971, when the United Nations General Assembly adopted a resolution "calling upon all athletes to refuse to participate in any sporting activity in countries officially applying a policy of racial discrimination or apartheid in the field of sports, and inviting national and international sports organizations which continue to organize sports meetings with South African teams to act in accordance with the present resolution". South African rugby, with its all-white national team (the Springboks), is clearly in the crosshairs.

In the past, the South African authorities have imposed their segregationist criteria on visiting national teams, as was the case with New Zealand. This measure imposed on the All Blacks, notably in 1959 during a tour of South Africa, which included Maori players, provoked a wave of public indignation on the New Zealand side and led to the cancellation of the tour. South Africa then amended its

---

31. BODIS Jean-Pierre, *Le rugby sud-africain. Histoire d'un sport en politique*, Karthala, 1995.

laws to ensure that home matches no longer caused controversy, allowing the Springboks to continue playing at international level. In the 1970s, rugby remained one of the few sports in which South Africa was represented at international level, and its national rugby team was even more widely perceived as a symbol of apartheid[32].

The Boycott Response to Apartheid

It was a (new) All Blacks tour of South Africa, a few months before the 1976 Games, that finally triggered one of the first major boycotts of the Olympics. A few days after the matches between South Africa and New Zealand, major demonstrations broke out in the Soweto district of Johannesburg in June 1976, as the black population took offence at a new law requiring Afrikaans, the language of the ruling white minority, to be taught as a second language. The demands turned into riots, which were severely repressed in bloodshed, with almost 300 people killed and several thousand injured.

The massacre had a strong international echo. The member countries of the Organization of African Unity (OAU) reacted, urging that all UN resolutions against the apartheid regime in South Africa be implemented. This includes all sporting disciplines. For the OAU, the All Blacks' tour of South Africa in the summer of 1976 was *de facto* tantamount to New Zealand violating the 1971 UN resolution and endorsing the South African apartheid regime. The OAU thus took four decisions, specifically concerning New Zealand's presence at the Montreal Olympics: condemnation of its links with South Africa,

---

32. See the chapter on South African rugby and apartheid in my book *Planète Rugby : 50 questions géopolitiques*, Max Milo, 2023.

an appeal to the IOC to prohibit the participation of the New Zealand delegation in the Games, an invitation to all OAU member states to boycott the Games if New Zealand took part, and an appeal to the international community to show solidarity with Africa[33]. These grievances were relayed by 16 African Olympic Committees to IOC President Lord Killanin, calling for New Zealand's definitive exclusion from the Games. If nothing is done, they will boycott the Games.

The IOC is thus faced with a situation similar to that of Rhodesia at the 1972 Olympic Games. Faced with the threat of a boycott, the Olympic organization had to exclude the African country, as the Rhodesian political regime also practiced a severe policy of racial segregation, including in its sports delegations. In 1976, the situation was different, as it was not South Africa's participation that was called into question. The IOC tried to defend its position and explain why it did not want to exclude New Zealand, which did not practice a policy of racial segregation and did not violate the Olympic Charter. The main justification: the All Blacks are indeed taking part in a tour of South Africa in defiance of UN resolutions, but rugby is not a sport of the Olympic movement. The IOC is therefore not competent to exclude the New Zealand Olympic delegation from the Games. The response was swift: faced with the absence of a decision, 22 African national delegations finally packed up and withdrew, a few hours before the start of the opening ceremony of the Montreal Olympics on July 17, 1976. Morocco, Cameroon and Egypt followed suit, withdrawing after just a few days of competition.

This event, right in the middle of this sporting concert of nations, will have a strong international impact, which will not be without

---

33. MONNIN Éric and MONNIN Catherine, « Le boycott politique des Jeux olympiques de Montréal », *Relations internationales*, 2008/2 (no. 134).

consequences. In 1977, the Commonwealth countries signed the Gleneagles Agreement, pledging to take all measures to discourage contact or competition between their nationals and sports organizations, teams or individuals from South Africa or any other racially segregated country. In the same year, the UN General Assembly adopts the "International Declaration against Apartheid in Sports".

Montréal 1976: A Microcosm of the World Geopolitical Scene

Apartheid was not the only political issue the IOC had to deal with at the Games. In early 1976, Canadian Prime Minister Pierre Trudeau bowed to pressure from the People's Republic of China (PRC), and issued an order prohibiting Taiwan from participating as "China" in the 1976 Montreal Olympic Games, even though this was technically the responsibility of the IOC. Refusing to comply with this requirement, which denied their distinct national identity, Taiwan opted to withdraw. This decision highlights the continuing dilemma of the "two Chinas", a conflict that dates back to the end of the Chinese civil war in 1949. The PRC thus intensified its lobbying during the 1970s to be recognized as the only "China" at international level, notably by taking Taiwan's seat on the UN Security Council in 1971. In sports, this culminated in the IOC's adoption of the Nagoya Resolution in 1979, which recognized the NOC of the PRC as the Chinese Olympic Committee and the NOC of the Republic of China as the "Chinese Taipei Olympic Committee"[34].

---

34. For more details, see chapter 14 on the Beijing 2008 Olympic Games.

Despite these geopolitical issues and an unprecedented mass boycott, the Montreal Games opened with 6,084 athletes from 92 nations, including 1,260 women. However, the celebration was tinged with sadness: the Israeli team wore black ribbons, a tribute to the athletes murdered in the 1972 Olympic bombing. The Canadian edition, however, saw sporting prowess in the shape of Romania's Nadia Comăneci, barely 14 years old, who rose to the rank of world icon. Her exceptional performance, crowned by seven perfect scores of 10, is an unprecedented feat in Olympic history. This sporting triumph transcended borders, and Nadia became a symbol of national pride in Romania, then under the yoke of Nicolae Ceaușescu's authoritarian regime. The Romanian regime, seeking to capitalize on Comăneci's success, conferred on her the title of "Hero of Socialist Labor", illustrating how Olympic victories are often recuperated for political propaganda purposes[35]. At the same time, the GDR, with 90 medals, including 40 gold, achieved a new performance, coming second in the medal table, behind the USSR, but above all ahead of the USA, which the East German regime would not fail to instrumentalize to validate its political model through sport.

In addition to this politicization of sport, the Montreal Games will above all be synonymous with organizational problems and cost inflation that will plunge the Canadian city into crisis for a long time to come. According to a study by Oxford University, the initial projected cost was $124 million, but the actual cost reached $1.5 billion, representing an overrun of 720%...[36] An overrun never

---

35. OLARU Stejarel, *Nadia Comaneci dans l'œil de la police secrète,* Robert Laffont, 2022.
36. BUDZIER Alexander, FLYVBJERG Bent, STEWART Allison, "The Oxford Olympics Study 2016: Cost and Cost Overrun at the Games", University of Oxford, July 2016.

before recorded in Olympic history. These economic and political difficulties plunged the Olympic movement into disarray. The very future of the Games was threatened, with two dreaded editions looming in the USSR in 1980 and the USA in 1984.

Chapter 11
- 1980 Moscow - 1984 Los Angeles: Boycott *vs.* Boycott: The Olympic Games at the Center of the Cold War

After the 1972 Munich Games, which were marred by the hostage-taking and assassination of Israeli athletes, the IOC was determined that the host city should be able to turn the page and put sport at the heart of the game. As we saw in the previous chapter, it was Montreal that had, to everyone's surprise, won the bid to host the 1976 Games, in the face of bids from the American and Soviet superpowers. In the face of this failure, they naturally positioned themselves for the organization of subsequent editions.

Olympism was an integral part of the Cold War and the ideological and political struggle between the two blocs. The organization of an Olympic event, which has grown in scope due to its television coverage and symbolic value, is also an instrument of power. However, a certain "détente" took hold in the 1970s, reflected in a series of agreements aimed at reducing tensions. These included the SALT agreements, which limited the nuclear armaments of the two superpowers. The vote to award the 1980 Olympic Games, for which the USSR (Moscow) and the USA (Los Angeles) have each submitted a bid, therefore promises to be less stormy than it might appear.

The Soviet authorities, with the organization of the Moscow Universiade in 1973[37], also prepared the ground and reassured the Olympic body of their ability to organize and host national delegations, even from the Western bloc. The United States was at a slight disadvantage, since in 1973 it was awarded the right to host another Olympic event in 1980, the Lake Placid Winter Games, which indirectly favored the Soviet camp. These various reasons partly explain why the IOC voted on October 23, 1974 in favor of Moscow over Los Angeles (39 votes to 20). With no previous Olympics held in the Eastern bloc, the hope of greater international cooperation through sport was strengthened. Similarly, the awarding of the 1984 Olympic Games to Los Angeles in 1978 reflects a certain reciprocity and the desire for the Olympics to serve as a vehicle for this détente[38].

---

37. The Universiade is an international multi-sport event organized for university athletes by the International University Sports Federation (FISU).
38. DUFRAISSE Sylvain, *Une histoire sportive de la guerre froide*, Nouveau Monde Éditions, 2023.

The USSR's Invasion of Afghanistan, the First Spark of the Boycott

However, two events were to change everything. In November 1979, the American hostage crisis in Iran marked a turning point. The hostage crisis followed the Iranian Revolution, which overthrew the Shah, an ally of the United States, and established an Islamic Republic under the leadership of Ayatollah Khomeini. The loss of American influence and the hostage crisis were seen as a humiliation on the American side, and President Jimmy Carter's policy of détente with his Soviet rival was criticized. On the Soviet side, the USSR invaded Afghanistan in December 1979. The aim of this intervention was to support the Afghan Communist government, threatened by internal insurrection. In so doing, the Soviet Union sought to secure its southern border and extend its influence in Central Asia. This action, perceived as a direct threat by the United States, marked a break in détente and signalled an intensification of the Cold War.

At the turn of the 1980s, Soviet power, having achieved nuclear parity with the United States and extended its influence with the installation of new missiles in Europe, represented an increasingly tangible threat to American hegemony. Against this backdrop of heightened rivalry, the Soviet invasion of Afghanistan was the spark that rekindled the flame of tension. The year 1980 was also marked by an American presidential election campaign, in which incumbent Democratic President Jimmy Carter found himself pitted against Republican Ronald Reagan. The latter, adopting a "peace through strength" stance, openly criticized Carter's policy of détente, arguing that it had enabled the USSR to gain ground both militarily and in its sphere of influence. The rise of Soviet power and the Iranian crisis contributed to a perception of weakness on the part of the Carter administration. These factors prompted Carter to raise his voice against the USSR and consider boycotting the Moscow Games. This was a way of regaining the initiative on the international stage and regaining popularity, just a few months before the start of the presidential campaign. On January 20, 1980, Carter issued an ultimatum to the Kremlin: "If in one month at the latest your troops have not evacuated Afghanistan, the American Olympic team will not go to Moscow, and we will ask other countries to abstain as well"[39].

The American camp was divided on the boycott issue. All the more so when an unexpected event occurred on February 22, 1980, during the Lake Placid Winter Olympics: the "Miracle on Ice"[40]. To everyone's surprise, the American ice hockey team won the gold medal after a narrow 4-3 victory over the Soviet team. This was quite a feat, given that the USSR had won the last 4 Olympic titles, and that little hope was given to a US team considered too young and inexperienced. This historic moment fueled the national debate on participation in the Moscow Olympics. For some, this sporting feat proved that direct confrontations with the Soviets, even on the sporting field, were an opportunity to demonstrate American superiority.

---

39. CARACCIOLI Tom, CARACCIOLI Jerry, *Boycott: Stolen Dreams of the 1980 Moscow Olympic Games*, New Chapter Press, 2008.
40. BURGAN Michael, *Miracle on Ice: How a Stunning Upset United a Country*, Compass Point Books, 2016.

> ### *The other US-USSR duel: the three seconds of the 1972 Munich Olympics*
>
> *The Munich basketball final on September 10, 1972, between the USA and the USSR, is one of the most controversial moments in the history of the Olympic Games, and fits perfectly into the tumultuous history of the Cold War.*
> *The United States has dominated Olympic basketball since the sport was introduced to the Olympic Games in 1936, winning every gold medal until 1972. The Munich final against the Soviet rival was therefore eagerly awaited. The match was marked by a series of controversial incidents, particularly in the final seconds.*
> *After a tight game, the USA lead 50-49. With three seconds left, the Soviets attempt a throw-in, but the referee stops the clock for reasons that are still disputed. After several questionable throw-ins, the Soviets make one last basket, winning the game 51-50. The American players immediately protest, refusing to recognize the validity of the result. Their protest was rejected by the Olympic Committee, and the Americans refused to mount the podium to receive their medals[41].*

A few months later, the United States, with the help of Secretary of State Henri Kissinger, pushed to invalidate the result. The IOC refused, and refused again and again. Even in 1992, when the USSR was dissolved, the American camp repeated its request to recover the gold medal. Even after the Cold War, these three seconds remain the longest in history.

---

41. MARTINEZ-DELCAYROU Thibaut, *Faute ! Dans les coulisses des plus grandes polémiques arbitrales*, Hugo Sport, 2022.

A Boycott that Doesn't Happen Overnight

The bloc logic of the Cold War might have led us to expect a united response from both East and West. However, the call for a boycott of the Moscow Olympics did not come automatically from America's allies. This resistance reflects the relative independence of the Olympic movement from political power. In the UK, despite Prime Minister Margaret Thatcher's call for a boycott, the final decision rested with the athletes and the British National Olympic Committee, the majority of whom chose to participate. In France, President Valéry Giscard d'Estaing adopted a hands-off approach, allowing an independent decision to be taken by the CNOSF (French National Olympic and Sports Committee), which sent a delegation to the USSR.

The debate was also intense in the USA, and it was not until April 1980, under strong political pressure from the Carter administration and economic players, that the US Olympic Committee voted in favor of the boycott, with 1,607 delegates in favor and 797 against[42]. The decision was motivated by a desire to condemn the USSR for its action in Afghanistan, and to signal a return to the Cold War game for the United States. Faced with American pressure to relocate the Games, the IOC decided, despite a major boycott in the offing, to hold the Olympic Games on Soviet soil.

---

42. "The 1980 Moscow Olympics Boycott", Wilson Center, February 27, 2017.

Moscow 1980: The Eastern Bloc Alone in Control

In the end, some 65 national delegations boycotted the Moscow Games, although only 80 countries took part, the lowest number since 1956. Among the notable national delegations absent were major delegations from the Western bloc, such as Canada, West Germany and Japan, as well as others such as China, in a bid to mark the difference between the Chinese Communist model and the Soviet model. The nations boycotting the event are not just a consequence of the Cold War bloc struggle. For example, 29 national delegations from Muslim countries did not travel to Moscow, as a direct reaction to the USSR's invasion of Afghanistan, in the sense that this military intervention was the first direct Soviet incursion into a "Third World" country, and a Muslim one at that.

Last but not least, some fifteen delegations boycotted at the very least. France did not take part in the opening ceremony, and competed under the Olympic flag rather than its national symbols. This was also the case for other Western bloc countries such as Italy, the Netherlands, Australia and New Zealand. During medal ceremonies, the Olympic anthem is played instead of the anthems of these countries, symbolically reinforcing their protest stance. Media coverage of the Games is significantly reduced in the West, with key broadcasters such as the USA and Japan choosing not to broadcast the competitions. This decision reduced the international impact of the Games and contrasted with the usual scope of the Olympics, even though it was a tremendous opportunity for the USSR to showcase its entire model.

Contrary to some expectations, the USSR and its allies, notably the GDR, did not use the Games excessively to promote their ideological model. However, the resounding success of these two nations at the Games, where they won a disproportionate share of the medals, nevertheless served as a demonstration of strength and sporting superiority: 195 for the USSR (including 8 gold medals for a single athlete, Alexander Dityatin), 126 for the GDR, while the third country on the podium, Bulgaria, won just 40. On the U.S. side, President Carter presented the 400 American athletes scheduled to take part in the Games with a medal, with these words: "Future generations will know what you did, not just in the sports archives, but in the history books. They will know that in 1980, you did more than anyone else in the world to hold high the banner of freedom and peace."[43]

Once again, the Olympics were an expression of political demands from the athletes themselves, despite the controlled framework of this Soviet edition. A duel in the pole vault between Poland's Władysław Kozakiewicz and the Soviet Union's Konstantin Volkov. The Polish pole vaulter received a hearty whistle from the public and, despite three successive failures, he secured the Olympic title by clearing a bar at 5.75m. After this jump, he concluded his performance with a victorious arm of honor to the audience at the Luzhniki stadium. A gesture that goes beyond the realm of sport. It was interpreted as a symbol of resistance to Soviet control of the "People's Democracies", at a time when Poland was in the grip of major internal political tensions. Indeed, this period shortly preceded the imposition of martial law by the Polish Communist regime in response to the movements of Solidarność, the first independent trade union in the Soviet bloc, calling for democratic reforms. Kozakiewicz's act

---

43. DUFRAISSE Sylvain, *Une histoire sportive de la guerre froide,* Nouveau Monde Éditions, 2023.

of defiance, against a Soviet rival to boot, is thus interpreted as a powerful symbol of Polish resistance and the wind of freedom that was brewing behind the Iron Curtain.

Los Angeles 1984: A Minimal Boycott of the Eastern Bloc

Given the scale of the boycott of the Moscow Games, one might have expected a certain reciprocity in the Soviet response to the Los Angeles Games, 4 years later. The response was not so automatic. It was primarily due to the hardening of American policy under the Reagan Doctrine. The Cold War had taken a new turn since the death of Soviet leader Leonid Brezhnev in 1982 and the election of U.S. President Ronald Reagan in 1981, whose slogan was *"Make America Great Again"*. The Reagan Doctrine was applied and expanded, through a strategy of providing official and unofficial support to guerrilla movements in Africa, Asia and Latin America, with the aim of overthrowing socialist regimes and reducing Soviet influence. The USSR, which was losing ground, asked itself the legitimate question of participating in these Olympics on American soil, in order to reaffirm the power of its model through its sporting successes.

The Soviet Union played for time and took the belated decision not to travel to the USA on May 8, 1984, two weeks before the athletes' registration deadline. The Soviet camp justified this decision by arguing that their athletes could not come to the United States for "security reasons, strong chauvinist feelings and anti-Soviet hysteria in the United States". However, Grigory Rodchenkov, former head of Russia's anti-doping laboratory, tells us that the *Politburo* took this decision because Los Angeles had refused access to its port to a Soviet ship, which was hiding a doping laboratory[44].

The USSR dragged fifteen other Eastern Bloc countries (GDR, Hungary, Poland, Czechoslovakia, Cuba, North Korea and Vietnam) with it, while Iran, Libya, Burkina Faso and Albania boycotted the Games out of ideological opposition to the USA. A number of Eastern Bloc countries on the bangs of the Soviet system neverthe-less decided to take part. Like Ceauşescu's Romania, which used sport as a means of promoting its political regime, and even fini-shed second in the medal table.

However, the boycott resulted in fewer absentees than in 1980, and the Games set a new record for participation: 140 nations, including 19 newcomers (from Bahrain to Djibouti, the Solomon Islands and Rwanda), and 6,829 athletes, including 1,556 women. In any case, this boycott strategy was far from relevant for the Soviet bloc, since, as at the Moscow Olympics, the absentees were not visible and could not demonstrate the social success of their model. The United States topped the medals table with 174 medals won, and American Carl Lewis's show of strength with 4 Olympic titles (100 m, 200 m, long jump and 4×100 m relay).

The Los Angeles Games are also seen as an organizational success, bringing the Games into a modern phase, thanks in particular to the support of numerous private sponsors, who made the Games profi-table and provided a new marketing opportunity. Thanks to the low construction costs, due to the use of existing sports infrastructures, coupled with the reliance on financing from private companies, the 1984 Games generated a profit of over 250 million dollars and

---

44. RODCHENKOV Grigory, *Dopage organisé*, Michel Lafon, 2021.

set the benchmark for the organization of future Olympic Games. The sporting event became a must-see event, and boycotts quickly became ineffective in the face of the international and media event that this theater of nations embodied.

Chapter 12 - 1992 Barcelona: The Games of "Reconciliation"?

The 1992 Olympic Games bring a wind of hope, given the period in which they are taking place. The previous Games, in Seoul in 1988, were the last to be marked by the East-West ideological divide, and also the first to feature the Paralympics in the same host city. Nevertheless, they enabled the USSR and its ally the GDR to dominate the Olympics for the last time, finishing 1st and 2nd respectively in the medal table. The collapse of the Soviet bloc, symbolized by the fall of the Berlin Wall on November 9, 1989, marked the end of this domination. Several factors contributed to this collapse, including the economic and political reforms (Perestroika and Glasnost) initiated by Soviet leader Mikhail Gorbachev. These reforms, aimed at modernizing the Soviet system, ultimately accelerated its disintegration by exposing its structural weaknesses and encouraging independence movements within the Soviet republics. The dissolution of the Soviet Union in December 1991 put an end to the Cold War and reshaped the global geopolitical landscape. The end of bipolar logic paved the way for an unprecedented international dynamic, characterized by aspirations for a new multipolar world order. The Barcelona Olympics will be the first major international event to materialize this.

Barcelona: A Choice Driven by Renewed Spanish Unity

But first, why are the Games being held in Barcelona? The selection of the Catalan city as host city in 1986 (among other candidates such as Paris, Belgrade and Birmingham) reflects the IOC's desire to recognize and promote Spain's entry into a modern era, following the gradual end of Franco's dictatorship from 1975 onwards. Barcelona's bid also served as a political tool. Spain's central government wanted to reconcile the country with its second city, and capital of the autonomous region of Catalonia, which had long been in opposition to Franco's regime and was demanding greater autonomy.

The Spanish government saw the Games as an opportunity to promote national unity, negotiating with Catalan leaders to authorize the display of Catalan symbols, while ensuring that there would be no political or pro-independence demonstrations during the event. 1992 was a banner year for Spain and the promotion of its cities and regions, with the organization of the Universal Exhibition in Seville and the designation of Madrid as European Capital of Culture. Nevertheless, this desire for Spanish unity through sport was called into question in the run-up to the Games, with the risk of attacks by the Basque nationalist group ETA[45].

---

45. BONIFACE Pascal, *JO politiques*, Éditions Eyrolles, 2016.

The Yugoslav Wars Come to the Games

With the fall of the Eastern bloc and the end of the Cold War, a new world seems to be emerging. The era of open, global conflict seemed to be over. This illusion was short-lived, however, with the outbreak of the Gulf War in 1990, when a coalition of states, led by the United States, intervened following Iraq's invasion of Kuwait. The IOC, however, tried to contribute to this idealistic vision by reviving the ancient tradition of the Olympic Truce for the Barcelona Summer Olympics. A pious dream that is about to be confronted with reality, notably the tensions in the Balkans.

After the collapse of the Soviet bloc, the Balkan region caught fire with the break-up of Yugoslavia. This multi-ethnic federation of six republics and two autonomous regions came into being in 1945. After following the Soviet communist model for a time, the Federal Republic of Yugoslavia broke with the USSR and maintained a policy of neutrality during the Cold War. Tito, the leader of Yugoslavia, was instrumental in extricating the country from Stalin's influence. This autopirate leader strongly united Yugoslavia, which he described as a federation "made up of six republics, five nations, four languages, three religions, two alphabets and a single party". When he died in 1980, after thirty-five years in power, the Yugoslav structure began to crumble, with the rise of nationalism in the various federated republics, long held in check by the central power in Belgrade.

The collapse of the USSR accelerated demands for greater autonomy, particularly in Eastern Europe, where many Communist regimes, satellites of Moscow, were overthrown. Yugoslavia was also affected. Nationalist tensions were exacerbated, leading to declarations of independence by Slovenia and Croatia in 1991, followed by Bosnia-Herzegovina in 1992. The response of Slobodan Milosevic's

Serbia, seeking to preserve Yugoslav unity under Serbian rule, led to a series of armed conflicts, resulting in the Yugoslav Wars. Following international recognition of Bosnian independence on April 6, 1992, Yugoslavia bombed the Bosnian capital, Sarajevo.

In response to the aggression and massive human rights violations, the UN adopts a series of sanctions against Yugoslavia. These sanctions are designed to isolate the Belgrade regime economically and politically, to halt the conflict and to promote a peaceful resolution of the crisis. The measures include an arms embargo, trade and financial restrictions, and the exclusion of Yugoslavia from various international institutions and events. Including sporting competitions[46]. The UN sanctions had a direct impact on the sporting world, preventing Yugoslav athletes from taking part in international competitions under their national flag, including the 1992 Olympic Games, which were only a few months away. However, the IOC managed to negotiate a compromise, allowing Yugoslav athletes to take part individually, under neutral symbols, in order to maintain the Olympic spirit while respecting the sanctions.

Bosnia-Herzegovina, Croatia and Slovenia, recently independent nations whose National Olympic Committees have been recognized by the IOC, are also taking part in the Barcelona Games, parading their new colors and symbols for the first time at the Opening Ceremony. The Croatian delegation stands out in particular thanks to its basketball team, led by Toni Kukoč, who, after an incredible run, takes the silver medal, beaten only by Michael Jordan's American "Dream Team".

---

46. Trégourès Loïc, *Le football dans le chaos yougoslave,* Non Lieu, 2019.

USSR, Germany, South Africa: The Post-Cold War Geopolitical Context Reflected in Sport

The Yugoslav case at the Barcelona Olympics is not the only reflection of post-Cold War international relations. This period of transition was significantly reflected in the composition of the participating nations, which reached a record 169, with 9,356 athletes (6,652 men and 2,704 women). Following the dissolution of the USSR in 1991, there was an urgent need for the IOC to determine how the former Soviet republics would participate in the next Winter Olympics in Albertville and the Summer Olympics in Barcelona in 1992. The IOC, anxious to maintain the Olympic spirit and allow athletes to participate, supported the idea of a "unified team". Twelve of the fifteen former Soviet republics of the USSR were united under a single Olympic banner, and celebrated their victories to the sound of the Olympic anthem, in the absence of shared national symbols.

Estonia, Latvia and Lithuania, meanwhile, managed to compete under their own flags, thus affirming their recently acquired independence and their break with the former Soviet giant. This unified team, in a final tribute to the Soviet sporting heritage, dominated the medal table with a total of 112 medals, including 45 golds, ahead of the United States (108 medals) and unified Germany (82 medals).

For the first time since the end of the Second World War, the German delegation took part as a unified team, with no distinction between West and East German athletes. The fall of the Berlin Wall led to the reunification of Germany, which took effect in October 1990. Sport, with the German team's victory at the 1990 World Cup and the participation of a single delegation at the Barcelona Games, was a powerful symbol of this reunification. A victory of unity over division, symbolizing the end of an era marked by ideological divisions between East and West.

The political transition led by Nelson Mandela also enabled South Africa to return to the Games, after 28 years of exclusion due to the apartheid policy. This is a significant decision, reflecting ongoing efforts to promote a peaceful transition. The South African presence in Barcelona, despite internal challenges and for the moment a limited number of athletes of color in this finally "mixed" delegation, is seen as a celebration of hope and a testament to sport's ability to serve as a bridge for reconciliation and social change. Powerful images from the Games will illustrate this, such as the fraternal embrace between Ethiopia's Derartu Tulu, the first black African female Olympic champion, and white South African Elena Mayer. Sport was a powerful instrument in this long process of reconciliation between the peoples of the "rainbow nation". The Springpoks' victory in the 1995 Rugby World Cup and Bafana Bafana's victory in the 1996 African Cup of Nations soccer tournament[47] were prime examples of this a few years later.

The Media and Economic Triumph of the Olympic Games

The Barcelona Olympic Games embody a further transition from a primarily sporting event to a global media and political mega-event. The Barcelona Games accelerated the transition from Olympism to the inclusion of professional athletes, notably with the

---

47. See the chapter on the 1995 Rugby World Cup in my book *Planète Rugby*, Max Milo, 2023.

appearance of NBA stars such as Michael Jordan, Magic Johnson and Larry Bird. The "Dream Team" dominated their opponents, winning every game by an average margin of 44 points and attracting immense media attention.

The end of the Cold War and the boom in communications technology meant that the Games were given unprecedented media coverage. More than 13,000 media outlets were accredited, exceeding the number of participating athletes, and broadcast rights reached $638 million, a 60% increase on the Seoul Games. The worldwide audience also exploded, rising from 2.5 billion viewers in 1988 to 3.5 billion in 1992, testifying to the event's growing appeal across the globe.

Finally, the organization of the Games has left a lasting legacy for the host city of Barcelona, radically transforming its urban landscape and tourist appeal. Massive investments in infrastructure, the renovation of the waterfront and the creation of sports and cultural facilities have transformed Barcelona into a modern, dynamic metropolis. This transformation will position the city as a leading tourist destination in the future, benefiting in the long term from its visibility and economic spin-offs. The Barcelona Olympics are estimated to have generated a direct impact of around 7 billion euros and an indirect impact of over 18 billion euros.

The Barcelona Olympics did more than mark the end of the Cold War. They also ushered in a new era for Olympism, characterized by greater integration of professional athletes, a media revolution and remarkable economic success for both the host city and the IOC. The combination of all these factors means that future editions of the Olympic Games will involve even more intense competition to host them. With new countries eager to reap the potential economic benefits and positive global media exposure of sport.

Chapter 13 - Sydney 2000:
Aborigines and Unified Korea: A New Dimension for the Opening Ceremony

"What happened tonight is a symbol. Something's going to change for Aborigines, people's attitudes on the street, political decisions... I know I've made a lot of people happy, whatever their life, whatever their story, and I'm happy to have achieved that too."[48] These were the words of Australian aboriginal athlete Cathy Freeman following her victory in the 400 m Olympic final on September 25, 2000. A symbolic achievement, since it was she who was chosen to light the Olympic flame at the opening ceremony of the Sydney Games, and who bore the full weight of Australia's national reconciliation.

---

48. WAWRZYNIAK Richard, *Histoire(s) des Jeux olympiques*, Mareuil Éditions, 2021.

The Aboriginal Context at the Center of the Arena

To understand this, we need to look at the Aborigines. They are the original inhabitants of Australia, present on the continent for over 50,000 years. Before the arrival of British settlers in the 18th century, these diverse peoples lived in perfect symbiosis with their environment, divided into hundreds of tribal groups, each with its own language and traditions. The arrival of British settlers in 1788 ushered in a period of profound turbulence for the Aborigines, marked by conflict, land expropriation and the introduction of deadly diseases. Successive colonial policies not only marginalized the Aboriginal community, but also severely hampered their access to their ancestral lands, language and culture.

Over the centuries, the Aborigines have been exploited and often forcibly removed from their ancestral lands. The Aboriginal condition slowly evolved under the pressure of militant movements, which succeeded in obtaining Australian citizenship for them in 1967. An Aboriginal flag was also created to partially recognize their belonging to this ancestral land. It wasn't until 1997 that the archives finally came to light, revealing that the Australian authorities had implemented policies that systematically removed children from their families to be raised by non-indigenous families or institutions, known as the "Stolen Generation". These policies were aimed at the forced assimilation of Aborigines into the dominant Western society, systematically erasing their culture and identity. The debate is therefore electric in the run-up to the Sydney Games, all the more so as the leaders of this indigenous people have announced that they intend to take advantage of the arrival of numerous journalists and tourists at the Games to denounce their current living conditions.

Australia did everything in its power to ease tensions. On September 15, 2000, the opening ceremony in Sydney became a powerful act of recognition for the Aboriginal peoples. In a stadium packed with 110,000 spectators and in front of millions of international television viewers, Cathy Freeman, silver medallist in the Atlanta 400 m, of Aboriginal origin and whose grandmother was part of this "stolen generation", stood facing the Olympic cauldron. When she lights the Olympic flame, this gesture goes beyond the simple act of sport to touch deeply with Australian identity and history. Recognition of the Aborigines at the Sydney Games was a response to both internal and external issues. Internally, the Australian government sought to right historical wrongs and promote national unity. Externally, Australia aimed to improve its international image. The years leading up to the Games had been marked by increasing criticism. By highlighting the culture and contributions of indigenous peoples, Australia wanted to demonstrate its commitment to human rights and cultural diversity, thereby strengthening its position on the world stage.

The Short-Lived Union of the Two Koreas

The opening ceremony was also marked by the entry of athletes from North and South Korea under the same banner. An event in itself, since the end of the Second World War and the Korean War (1950-1953), the Korean peninsula has been divided into two distinct and often antagonistic entities: the Democratic People's Republic of Korea (North Korea) and the Republic of Korea (South Korea). The division resulted not only in one of the most heavily fortified militarized borders in the world, but also decades of mistrust and intermittent tensions, punctuated by periods of relative détente.

The idea of a unified Olympic entry for the two Koreas has been a complex diplomatic initiative, orchestrated mainly by the IOC and its President Juan Antonio Samaranch. Since the 1990s, the IOC has actively promoted initiatives to use Olympism and sport as a means of bringing divided nations closer together. After months of dialogue and compromise, a historic agreement was reached[49]. Athletes from both Koreas would parade together under a "unification flag", a white-backed flag with a blue map of the unified Korean peninsula, symbolizing the hope of peace and reconciliation. The joint participation of the two Koreas in the Sydney Olympic Games had a significant impact on the international perception of the possibilities for peace on the Korean peninsula. It showed that, despite persistent challenges and deep-seated ideological differences, there is room for rapprochement and mutual understanding. The event also underlined the new importance of the Olympic Games opening ceremony, which, thanks to its mediatization, can facilitate diplomatic dialogue.

A New Participation Record, Illustrated by the Media Coverage of Eric Moussambani

Following this symbolically charged ceremony, a record 199 nations entered the stadium to take part in the Parade of Nations. The only missing IOC member was Afghanistan, banned because of the

---

49. Thilou Thomas, *Histoire(s) de Jeux : Les Jeux Olympiques de 1896 à 2021, 125 ans d'Humanité*, L'Harmattan, 2022.

extremist Taliban regime and their desire to prohibit Afghan women from taking part in sporting competitions. Eritrea, Micronesia, Palau and East Timor take part in their first Games. The four athletes from East Timor are taking part as individual Olympians, marching directly in front of the host country. This situation is explained by the conflict between Indonesia and Timorese independence forces since 1975, which ended in 1999 with a UN-sponsored act of self-determination. Which explains why, here too, the IOC has positioned itself as an organization capable of illustrating, through sport, situations of peace. East Timor's NOC was subsequently recognized by the IOC, and the country began competing under its own colors at the 2004 Olympic Games.

In terms of competition, the medal table was dominated by the USA (93 medals, including 37 gold), closely followed by Russia (89), with China (59) and Australia (58) a little further back. Above all, nearly 80 NOCs won medals, a record number. Among the 10,647 participating athletes (6,579 men, 4,068 women), one in particular stood out, not for his sporting prowess, but for the simple fact of taking part: Eric Moussambani. The swimmer from Equatorial Guinea took part in the 100-meter freestyle event. Moussambani caught the world's attention not for a medal, but for his anti-record time of 1 minute 52 seconds and 72 hundredths, well short of the world record of 47 seconds and 84 hundredths. Despite her difficulties, her courage and perseverance won the hearts of the public and the media. Her effort, in an Olympic pool for the first time in her life, was greeted by a resounding ovation from the Australian public, who chanted her first name as she performed.

This scene was widely reported and exalted as the embodiment of the Olympic spirit, reminding us that the Games are also a celebration of participation, personal effort and courage, as much as of victory and records. The media highlighted the contrast between his performance and that of elite athletes, while praising his audacity to compete against the best, despite limited resources and training. Above all, Moussambani's situation, admitted to the Olympic Games without meeting the minimum qualification requirements, illustrates how the IOC plays a role as an international player in encouraging the participation of developing countries lacking comprehensive training facilities. The Olympic Games thus represent a platform for promoting athletes and countries that have little chance of being seen outside of this moment, thus reinforcing the "universal" reach of Olympism.

CHAPTER 14 - BEIJING 2008: DEMONSTRATING CHINESE SUPERPOWER

In 2008, China is hosting the Olympic Games, clearly demonstrating its ambition to present itself as a rising superpower on the world stage. The selection of Beijing as host city was the result of a deliberate strategy to demonstrate China's economic, technological and cultural power. With an investment of nearly 44 billion dollars, China has built and renovated 37 sports facilities, including the iconic "Bird's Nests" and the "Water Cube", transforming the Beijing Games into a spectacular showcase of Chinese progress and entry into the court of the great powers. This demonstration aims to reinforce China's international stature, symbolizing its evolution from a predominant regional player to a leading global power[50].

After an unsuccessful bid for the 2000 Olympics (narrowly losing out to Sydney by 45 votes and Beijing by 43), China's bid won out over rival cities such as Toronto, Paris, Istanbul and Osaka in the 2001 IOC vote. This victory represented an opportunity for the IOC to open up its flagship event to a new territory and to the world's

---

50. Augustin Jean-Pierre, Gillon Pascal, *Les jeux du monde. Géopolitique de la flamme olympique*, Armand Colin, 2021.

most populous country at the time, and to use the occasion to stimulate the development of sport in Asia.

China's Contrasting History with the Olympics

China, with its thousand-year-old civilization, has gone through periods of greatness and decline. The "century of humiliation" (1839-1949), marked by foreign invasions and civil wars, profoundly affected the country. After the founding of the People's Republic of China in 1949, the country embarked on a long road of reconstruction and modernization. The economic reforms launched by Deng Xiaoping in the late 1970s enabled China to open up to the world and enjoy rapid economic growth.

However, China had to wait to organize its first Games, as this reflects a contrasting trajectory within the Olympic movement. The controversy surrounding China's representation at the Olympic Games has its roots in the political division between the People's Republic of China (PRC) and the Republic of China, now known as Taiwan. The Communist victory in the Chinese Civil War of 1949 led to the founding of the PRC by Mao Zedong. At the same time, Chiang Kai-shek's nationalists took refuge on the island of Taiwan, formerly under Japanese control, and saw themselves as the legitimate representatives of China. This division creates the unique situation of two governments claiming the name "Republic of China", each with its own territorial claims and political vision for China's future. The IOC tried to ignore geopolitical considerations and invited both NOCs to the 1952 Helsinki Olympics. The PRC took part, but Taiwan, then the "Republic of China", refused to participate. From 1958 to 1976, it was the PRC that boycotted the Games because of the recognition of Taiwan's participation.

The early 1970s marked a crucial period of diplomatic openness for China. An emblematic moment in this opening-up was the recovery by the PRC of the seat of permanent member of the UN Security Council, until then held by Taiwan, in 1971. This change was made possible by UN General Assembly Resolution 2758, adopted on October 25, 1971, which recognized the PRC as "the sole legitimate representative of China" at the UN. This resolution, supported by a majority of member countries, reflected a significant shift in global geopolitical alliances and recognition of China's growing importance on the international stage. This diplomatic turning point is part of the broader context of the policy of reform and opening-up initiated by the Chinese regime in the 1970s. One of the most symbolic events of this period was US President Richard Nixon's historic visit to China in 1972, marking the start of a new era of Sino-American relations after decades of hostility.

In 1979, under the aegis of Deng Xiaoping's new policy of reform and opening-up, China began negotiations with the IOC to reintegrate the Olympic Games, while continuing the diplomatic battle with Taiwan. The Nagoya resolution, approved in November 1979, stipulated that the PRC Olympic Committee would be officially designated as the "Chinese Olympic Committee", using all the national symbols of the People's Republic of China (PRC)[51]. This decision was part of a wider effort by Beijing to reintegrate international institutions and improve its diplomatic relations, particularly with the West. With this decision, the Olympic movement also succeeded in getting the PRC and Taiwan to coexist on

---

51. BONIFACE Pascal, *JO politiques*, Éditions Eyrolles, 2016.

the same ground. Although Taiwan is no longer a member of the UN due to opposition from the PRC, the Taiwanese NOC is maintained within the Olympic movement under the name of "Chinese Taipei Olympic Committee". This compromise satisfies Beijing, as it affirms that Taiwan is an integral part of Chinese territory, while allowing Taipei to retain an international presence, albeit under a modified name and symbols.

China made its Olympic comeback with the 1984 Olympic Games in Los Angeles, and went on to establish itself as a major sporting power, culminating in the organization of the 2008 Games in Beijing. This Olympiad should provide an unprecedented demonstration of China's ability to organize a major world event, reflecting its economic ascent and its ambition to play a leading international role.

Tibet, Human Rights and Boycotts: the Beijing Olympics in Turmoil

However, Beijing has not seen the last of its surprises: in the run-up to the Games, there has been much criticism and protest around the world, particularly concerning China's authoritarian regime, human rights and press freedom. The situation in Tibet also dominates the media agenda. In March 2008, demonstrations in Lhasa and other Tibetan regions calling for independence or greater autonomy from China were violently suppressed. This rekindled international calls for a boycott of the Games, exacerbating tensions between China and several Western countries. Tibet, annexed by China in 1950, is a region whose management by China is regularly criticized for infringing the rights of Tibetans and their culture. Coverage of these events by foreign journalists is severely hampered by restrictions imposed by the Chinese government, despite promises of press freedom made in connection with the Games. These limitations are drawing criticism from many governments and non-governmental organizations, who point the finger at the lack of transparency and freedom in the country[52].

As for the question of a boycott, it is being seriously considered by several countries, notably the United States, the United Kingdom and France, where influential voices in political and civil spheres are calling for the Games to be used as a means of putting pressure on China. Among the leaders opting not to take part in the opening ceremony are British Prime Minister Gordon Brown and German Chancellor Angela Merkel. The then President of the United States, George W. Bush, attended the Games, but expressed concerns about the human rights situation in China prior to his arrival. This diplomatic boycott was intended to signal disapproval of the Chinese government's policies without completely disengaging from diplomatic and trade relations with China. This shows that the "weapon" of boycott is now difficult to apply, given that the Olympics are about more than just sport.

The start of the Games was also marked by another event: for the first time in the history of the Olympic Games, a war broke out between two participating nations: Russia launched a military offensive against Georgia because of the situation in South Ossetia. The conflict began on August 8, 2008, the very day of the opening ceremony of the Beijing Games. This territorial conflict exacerbated international tensions and drew attention to the conflicting

---

52. "Olympic Torch's Tibet Visit is Short and Political", *The New York Times*, June 22, 2008.

relations between Russia and Georgia. A noteworthy moment of the Games occurred during the medal ceremony for the women's 10-meter shooting final, on August 10, 2008. Russian silver medallist Natalia Paderina and Georgian bronze medallist Nino Salukvadze exchanged a warm embrace, symbolizing the Olympic spirit despite the ongoing conflict. However, the conflict persists, demonstrating that, despite the utopian idea of an Olympic truce, the Olympic Games are no exception to the rule.

Demonstrating China's Superpower

During the Games, China won an impressive 100 medals, 48 of them gold, surpassing the United States, which had 112 medals, but only 36 gold. This is a significant achievement, as for the first time since the end of the Cold War, the USA does not lead the medal table at the Olympic Games. Among the highlights was the performance of American swimmer Michael Phelps, who broke seven world records on his way to winning eight gold medals. However, Jamaican sprinter Usain Bolt also stole the show, setting new world records in the 100 m and 200 m, becoming the world's fastest man in front of billions of spectators.

China's victory on the medal table is not just a question of numbers; it reflects a deliberate strategy of sports development and investment in infrastructure and athlete training, which began decades before the 2008 Games. This strategy is an integral part of China's *soft power* policy, aimed at improving its global image[53].

---

53. GUOQUI XU, *Olympic Dreams: China and Sports, 1895-2008*, Harvard University Press, 2008.

By succeeding in staging a major global event without any notable hindrance, and by excelling in a number of disciplines, China has demonstrated its ability to compete on all fronts with the world's greatest powers, notably the USA. The sporting competition between China and the United States has thus only just begun, and this battle for sporting supremacy is a new playing field in the struggle for influence to claim the position of the world's leading power.

CHAPTER 15 - 2016 - RIO: OLYMPIC RECOGNITION FOR KOSOVO

The 2016 Olympic Games in Rio de Janeiro represent a first for Brazil and for the Olympic world. They are the first to be held in South America. They are also the first Summer Games to be held during the host country's winter season. The event also marked the return of the Games to the southern hemisphere, and the first Olympiad under Thomas Bach's presidency of the IOC. The selection of Rio de Janeiro as host city for the 2016 Games, announced in 2009, was seen as a historic and strategic decision by the IOC. Several factors contributed to this choice. Firstly, the IOC wanted to diversify the Olympic Games geographically and reinforce their universal character by staging them in South America for the first time. The choice of Rio thus marked a new stage in the inclusivity and accessibility of the Olympic Games worldwide. Secondly, as Brazil is one of the world's leading emerging economies, belonging to the BRIC group (Brazil, Russia, India, China), hosting the Games represented recognition of its growing weight on the world stage. For the IOC, it was an opportunity to establish a foothold in a region undergoing rapid economic and demographic growth, while promoting the Olympic values of diversity and international cooperation.

The selection of Rio as host city generated national enthusiasm and immense pride for Brazil, and contributed to a cycle of international visibility through sport, following the 2014 Football World Cup on home soil. However, preparations are soon overshadowed by a series of challenges and controversies. The country is going through a serious economic and political crisis, including impeachment proceedings against President Dilma Rousseff and major corruption scandals that are splashing many strata of Brazilian society. Another problematic aspect concerns environmental management, in particular the pollution of Guanabara Bay, where sailing events are held. Despite initial promises, efforts to clean up the bay are falling short of expectations, exposing athletes to deplorable conditions. In addition, the Zika virus epidemic is causing worldwide concern, although ultimately no cases are reported among participants and spectators[54].

In economic terms, the Rio Games are seen as a showcase for Brazil's dynamism and capacity for innovation. An initial budget of $14.4 billion is allocated to the construction and renovation of 37 sports facilities, with the hope of stimulating the local economy and improving urban infrastructure. However, the final costs reached around $20 billion, including spending on security and infrastructure. This cost inflation has led to criticism of financial management and the use of public funds. The legacy of the Rio Games remains mixed. Several venues built for the Games are suffering from under-utilization or post-Games abandonment.

---

54. GATINOIS Claire, « Pollution, village olympique en chantier... À Rio, les Jeux sont (mal) faits », Le Monde.fr, August 3, 2016.

The president of the Brazilian Olympic Committee, Carlos Arthur Nuzman, will also be publicly accused of "bribing" leaders of other countries for the choice of Rio. All of which further tarnishes this Brazilian edition, particularly in terms of the country's positive international image.

The Origins of Kosovo's Historic Participation

11,238 athletes from 206 national delegations[55] took part in the 2016 Games, with the USA dominating the medal table (121), ahead of Great Britain (67) and China (70). However, the British delegation won more gold medals, confirming the positive effects orchestrated by its sports policy in the run-up to the London 2012 Olympic Games. Another country won a gold medal that goes beyond sport: Kosovo. After declaring its independence from Serbia in 2008, this country is taking part in the Olympic Games for the first time in 2016.

What is the situation in Kosovo? Kosovo is a Central European territory of some 10,000 km² (the size of the Gironde département), landlocked between Albania, Northern Macedonia, Montenegro and Serbia. Kosovo's history is a complex one, intimately linked to that of its Albanian and Serbian neighbors. In 1878, at the Berlin Congress of Nations, the Kingdom of Serbia became independent and was granted the territory of present-day Kosovo. In the Serbian imagination, this land is associated with the battle of Kosovo Polje

---

55. A team of "Independent Olympic Athletes" competed at these Games. The team was made up of Kuwaiti athletes who competed under the Olympic flag, as the Kuwaiti NOC had been suspended by the IOC due to government interference.

on June 15, 1389, or the battle of the "Field of Blackbirds", which saw the Ottoman Empire clash with a coalition of Christian princes, notably from Serbia. This battle founded the myth that Kosovo was the cradle of the Serbian nation.

During the Second World War, Kosovo became part of Albania, then under the control of Fascist Italy. After the war and the creation of the Eastern bloc under the aegis of the USSR, Tito, the Yugoslav Communist leader, intended to create a federation of the various Balkan countries, the Socialist Federal Republic of Yugoslavia. This antagonized USSR leader Stalin, who wanted to control all the countries of Eastern Europe. In 1948, the break between the Soviet and Yugoslav states was complete. Relations were severed. Albania joined the ranks of the "People's Democracies", while Kosovo was integrated into Yugoslavia as an autonomous province.

After Tito's death in 1980, the first nationalist demonstrations broke out in this large federation. Kosovo, with its majority Albanian population, wanted to become a republic in its own right. Yugoslavia's Communist rulers, influenced by the Republic of Serbia and its leader Slobodan Milošević, disagreed and harshly repressed the riots. With the collapse of the USSR, from 1989 onwards, many Eastern Bloc nations fought for their independence, causing a snowball effect within the Yugoslav Federal Republic: several of its members demanded independence. This was the case for Slovenia, Croatia and Bosnia. Slobodan Milošević's Serbia tried by force to save what remained of the federation, triggering the bloody Yugoslav wars. The Dayton Accords of 1995 put an end to this inter-ethnic fighting and to the great federation of Yugoslavia, which is now made up of Serbia, Montenegro and Kosovo.

However, the new republic was not finished with the war, as independence aspirations began to emerge in the south. In 1998, a new war broke out in Kosovo between Albanian separatists and Serbian forces, resulting in over 13,000 deaths and mass emigration. NATO intervention in 1999 put an end to the armed conflict and to Milošević's repressive, violent regime. Kosovo remained a territory of undetermined status until 2007. It was not until then that former Finnish President Martti Ahtisaari, who was overseeing negotiations between the Serbian and Kosovar governments, submitted a proposal to the United Nations Security Council to grant Kosovo the status of an independent state. Russia, a permanent member of the Council, vetoed the resolution on the grounds that independence would be contrary to the principle of territorial unity of its Serbian ally. However, Kosovo did not wait for UN approval, and unilaterally declared its independence on February 17, 2008[56].

Sports Representation: Kosovo's Response to Disputed Independence

Since then, a long diplomatic battle has been waged to have Kosovo recognized as such. By September 4, 2020, (approximately) 98 of the 193 members of the United Nations had recognized Kosovo's independence, including the United States, France and Germany. Although present in several international organizations (IMF, World Bank), the new Kosovar state is not part of one of the

---

56. CATTARUZZA Amaël, SINTÈS Pierre, *Atlas géopolitique des Balkans*, Autrement, 2016.

most important, the UN, due to the Russian veto. Russia and Serbia are not the only countries fiercely opposed to recognizing Kosovo as a state. This is also the case for China and Spain, for whom recognition of this independence would send a positive signal to the supporters of strong regionalist claims within their borders (Tibet and Xinjiang in China, Basque Country and Catalonia in Spain). As for Serbia, it has been waging a major diplomatic campaign since 2017 to get certain states to restrict visas for Kosovar nationals.

Faced with these challenges, Kosovo is looking for other ways to exist and gain recognition on the international stage, notably through membership of major sports organizations. Recognition by the IOC is particularly important for Kosovo, as it gives it media and symbolic representation on a par with other internationally recognized states. In 2014, the IOC officially recognized the NOC of Kosovo, enabling the country to participate in the Olympic Games for the first time in 2016[57]. Participation in the Olympic Games is crucial for Kosovo for several reasons. Olympic participation enhances Kosovo's international stature. By competing under their country's flag, Kosovar athletes become symbols of independence and national sovereignty. At the Rio 2016 Games, Majlinda Kelmendi, a Kosovar judoka, became an emblematic figure by winning the first Olympic gold medal. This triumph was seen not only as a sporting victory, but also as an affirmation of Kosovar national identity on the world stage. An international affirmation thanks to sport, which continues with two further gold medals in judo at the Tokyo 2021 Olympic Games.

---

57. GAUTIER Florian, « Le sport, nouvelle vitrine du Kosovo », *Le Monde diplomatique*, February 2016.

The Refugee Olympic Team

For the first time in history, the 2016 Rio Games will see the participation of the Refugee Olympic Team. This IOC initiative, with the support of the United Nations High Commissioner for Refugees (UNHCR), aims to provide a platform for athletes displaced by conflict and persecution, as well as for those who are unable to train in their home countries.

The Olympic flag and the Olympic anthem are used as team symbols. These athletes represent the more than 100 million displaced people in the world. This initiative is being renewed for the Tokyo 2021 Olympics, as well as for Paris 2024, where 36 athletes from 11 different countries of origin, mainly Afghanistan, Iran and Syria, will be present.

The Refugee Olympic Team highlights the courageous stories of these athletes, while raising awareness among billions of viewers of the difficult conditions faced by refugees around the world. It's an extremely political team, given the many contexts and persecutions surrounding the stories of each of these athletes.

Chapter 16 - Paris 2024: A Geopolitical Challenge for France

The Paris 2024 Olympic Games are more than just a sporting event. Now followed by almost half the planet, they offer unparalleled visibility for the host city, but above all for the country itself. The Olympic Games are a testament to a country's ability to organize a major world event, while welcoming over 200 national delegations. Given the global visibility and symbolic prestige of the event, more and more countries are seeking to host the Olympics. In particular, the new emerging powers are using the Olympics as a means of materializing their economic progress, their brand image and their entry into the world's big league. Countries accustomed to organizing sporting events, for the most part in the Western world due to their Olympic heritage, are not to be outdone, since the Olympic Games are a major opportunity to bring together, in a defined period and territory, all the world's attention, while at the same time promoting their *soft power.* It is these ambitions, in particular, that have prompted countries such as France to renew their bid to host a new edition of the Olympic Games.

France's Diplomatic Battle to Win the Olympic Games

As we have seen, securing the organization of the Olympic Games has been a geopolitical issue since its inception in 1896. This competition was reinforced by the Cold War in the 1970s and 1980s, and reached a new stage with the "commodification" of the Games in the 2000s, when the new emerging powers (notably China, Russia and Brazil) made the organization of an Olympic event a strategic demonstration objective. The established powers, for their part, must remain in the race to organize such sporting events in order to preserve a certain stature and international influence.

After two editions of the Olympic Games on home soil (1900, 1924), France bid for a third edition at the end of the 20th century, but it was Spain and the city of Barcelona that won the 1992 Games. At the beginning of the 21st century, the battle was even fiercer. Following the success of the 1992 and 1996 editions for the "host countries", many countries were keen to organize the Games. The IOC, for its part, set out to open up the event to new countries, and established a certain rotation of continents for the host city, thus limiting the number of European editions. This was one of the reasons why China and Beijing were awarded the 2008 Olympic Games in 2001, rather than Paris, Istanbul, Osaka and Toronto. This opens up the Olympics to new destinations and new horizons.

France is not giving up and is still aiming to organize the Games, with the 2012 edition in its sights. Competition is fierce with Spain (Madrid), the United States (New York), Russia (Moscow) and the United Kingdom (London). The French and British bids were ahead of the competition, but at the IOC session in Singapore on July 6, 2005, after a close four-round vote, it was London that came out on top, ahead of Paris by just four votes. In the weeks following this vote, members of the French delegation claimed that the London delegation had violated the rules, particularly in terms of lobbying by the then Prime Minister, Tony Blair. These accusations carried considerable weight at a time when the IOC was already reeling from the corruption and bribery scandal surrounding the award of the 2002 Winter Olympics to Salt Lake City. However, the Olympic body quickly reacted by rejecting the accusations and asserting that the competition had been fair. For Sebastian Coe, chairman of the British bid committee, the explanation for the French defeat lay elsewhere, as he explained to a member of the French delegation: "The French bid was exceptional, perhaps the best in the competition, but you lost because you didn't ask yourselves why you should organize the Games. You never explained what the Games would achieve, what they would represent as a legacy, as transformations for your country and as an appeal to the Olympic spirit in general"[58].

Mistakes that won't be repeated for the 2024 Olympic bid, where sport and heritage are given greater prominence. Circumstances were more favorable, however, as Hamburg, Rome and Budapest withdrew from the race, leaving Paris and Los Angeles as the only candidate cities. From 2016 onwards, IOC President Thomas Bach considered a double award, explaining that there were "too many losing bids". Finally, on September 13, 2017, the IOC unanimously decides to award the 2024 and 2028 Games simultaneously. The United States agreed to position itself for 2028, leaving the initiative to France for the 2024 edition. The French capital thus becomes the second city, after London, to host the Summer Olympics for the third time: 1900, 1924 and now 2024.

---

58. WAWRZYNIAK Richard, *Histoire(s) des Jeux olympiques*, Mareuil Éditions, 2021.

Paris 2024: A Key Event for French *Soft Power*

With these Games, France must demonstrate to the international community its ability to organize and manage an event of this scale. This implies modern infrastructures, controlled security and efficient management of the flow of visitors, athletes and international delegations. In the run-up to this mega-event, the budget for the Paris Olympics, originally announced at 6.6 billion euros, has risen to 9 billion euros, of which 2.4 billion will come from public funds. Nevertheless, the Olympics are still a long way from the $30-40 billion budget of the Beijing edition, and the total cost of the French edition is expected to be in a fairly similar range to that of the London 2012 Games (11 billion euros). France hopes to distinguish itself through more rigorous financial management, as well as a more lasting legacy.

Although Paris 2024 can draw on pre-existing sports venues, the organization has put sustainability at the heart of its approach, so as not to repeat the "white elephants" of Athens in 2004 or Rio in 2016, i.e. the many new structures built that were then underused or left to decay. France's strategy is therefore to think of the organization and construction of these Olympic Games as an urban gas pedal and not just as a sporting event. As such, Paris 2024 is committed to significantly reducing the carbon footprint of the Games, aiming for a 55% reduction in greenhouse gas emissions compared to previous games. The French organization is also seeking to capitalize on emblematic sites, such as the Stade de France, the Grand Palais and the Château de Versailles, to promote France's heritage and image internationally.

The Olympic Games will therefore remain a powerful tool of *soft power, i.e.* their ability to influence others through attraction and persuasion rather than coercion. The world's biggest sporting mega-event is an ideal platform for promoting culture, lifestyle and values on the international stage. The opening and closing ceremonies, especially the one on the Seine, as well as the parallel cultural events, will showcase French art, music and heritage, reinforcing the country's cultural appeal and *nationbranding*. With an expected global audience of 5 billion viewers, the impact on France's visibility will be significant, particularly over the long term. It remains to be seen whether there will be enough positive spin-offs, particularly economic ones, to justify the organization of such a mega-event in the eyes of the population, but also of future candidate countries.

What are the "Positive" Spin-Offs for France?

Paris 2024 is expected to generate substantial economic benefits, with 15 million tourists expected, comparable to those seen at previous editions, such as London in 2012. In London, the Olympic Games generated around $23 billion in economic benefits, including the creation of thousands of jobs and a significant increase in the number of foreign visitors. In 2013, the year following the Games, London recorded a 6% increase in foreign visitors, reaching 33 million.

Paris hopes to capitalize on this opportunity in a similar way. The French capital, with its rich cultural and historical heritage, aims to reinforce its position as a leading tourist destination. Barcelona, for example, saw its tourist numbers quadruple after the 1992 Olympic Games, and continues to benefit from improved infrastructure and increased international renown. France hopes that the 2024 Games will have a similar long-term effect, attracting visitors and boosting tourism revenues.

According to an economic impact study carried out by CDES (Centre de droit et d'économie du sport), forecasts indicate that the Paris 2024 Olympic Games could generate between 6.7 and 11.1 billion euros in direct and indirect economic spin-offs for the Paris region[59]. This includes not only tourism revenues, but also infrastructure investment, job creation and increased tax revenues. However, it is crucial to remain cautious about these projections. Studies of previous editions of the Olympic Games have shown that economic impacts can sometimes be overestimated. For example, while London 2012 was able to leverage the event to revitalize parts of the city, attract investment and make it an economic success, other cities have struggled to monetize post-event infrastructure[60].

Paris 2024: The Security Challenge in a Tense Geopolitical Context

Historically, major international sporting events, such as the Games, are times when maximum security is required due to the concentration of populations and the presence of important figures, such as numerous heads of state and diplomatic delegations. Reminiscences of past tragedies, such as the bombing of the 1972 Munich Olympics, remind us that even athletes can be prime targets for a political message.

---

59. CDES - Update of the Paris 2024 economic impact study, May 14, 2024.
60. AUGUSTIN Jean-Pierre, GILLON Pascal, *Les jeux du monde. Géopolitique de la flamme olympique*, Armand Colin, 2021.

In particular, this echoes the major geopolitical tensions in 2024, notably those of the Russian-Ukrainian conflict and the Israeli-Palestinian conflict. The participation of Russian and Belarusian athletes under a neutral banner remains a controversial issue, heightening security and political concerns. The recent conflict between Israel and Hamas adds a further layer of risk, with potential threats of violence during the Games. This raises an additional security challenge, especially as France, particularly since the Paris attacks in 2015, has stepped up its anti-terrorism measures and continues to improve its security protocols for major international sporting events, through Euro 2016 and the Rugby World Cup 2023.

The organization of the Paris Games must maneuver between the desire to celebrate unity through sport and the need to recognize political realities. The Olympic truce, although promoted by the IOC and adopted at the UN, remains illusory since conflicts will persist and past examples, such as at the 2008 Olympics or the 2014 Winter Olympics, have shown that this truce can blithely be broken or disregarded. The success of the 2024 Olympic Games, which for the first time have perfect parity, with as many male as female athletes taking part, will therefore depend not only on France's know-how in organizing international events, but also on the political and international context surrounding the event. Once again, the Olympic Games will be analyzed as a major geopolitical arena.

CHAPTER 17 - PARIS 2024: RUSSIA-UKRAINE

The Paris 2024 Olympic Games are taking place in a particularly tense geopolitical context, deeply marked by the ongoing repercussions of the war between Russia and Ukraine. This conflict has significant implications not only on the political and military terrain, but also in international sporting competitions, transforming sport into a symbolic and diplomatic battlefield. The French Olympiad is a further demonstration of this.

Act I: The War in Ukraine and the IOC's Recommendation to Exclude Athletes Representing Russia

February 24, 2022 marked the start of the war in Ukraine, following Vladimir Putin's Russian military offensive on Ukrainian territory. The violence of this aggression and the international reactions of the United States and its European and Western allies led to fears of the worst, namely that this conflict, on Europe's doorstep, would lead to escalation and a third world war. International reactions were swift, both economic and political. Sport also got involved, with the IOC recommending on February 28, 2022 that international sports federations exclude Russian (and Belarusian, Russia's allies) athletes, teams and officials from their competitions. This measure was quickly adopted by various sporting bodies, such as FIFA, which excluded Russia from the 2022 World Cup qualifiers, and UEFA, which banned Russian clubs and national teams from its European competitions.

These sanctions are designed to further isolate Russia on the international stage, putting pressure on Vladimir Putin's government to halt its military actions. This limitation of Russian expression on the sporting stage is by no means anecdotal. Ever since he took power in 2000, Putin has made it a strategic element in his bid to enhance Russia's image on the international stage and restore it to its Soviet-era stature. Over the years, Putin has created a system described by geopolitician Lukas Aubin as a "sportokratura": a "politico-economic-sports system involving oligarchs, politicians and sportsmen has been implemented to create an extremely successful sports model"[61], *i.e.* one that uses political, economic and sports relays to promote, through sport, Russia's return to the forefront after the fall of the Soviet bloc. This strategy will be particularly successful in the 2010 decade, with the organization of the Winter Olympics in Sochi in 2014 and the Football World Cup in Russia in 2018.

However, this politico-sports strategy will be undermined from 2014 onwards following the revelations by Grigory Rodchenkov, former head of Russia's national anti-doping laboratory, about the

---

61. AUBIN Lukas, *La sportokratura sous Vladimir Poutine*, Bréal, 2022.

Russian state doping system[62], which leads to Russia's suspension from numerous international competitions, including the Tokyo 2021 Olympics (although we will see later that this will not actually be the case). Sporting sanctions following the war in Ukraine go even further, as the major international federations effectively exclude Russian athletes and teams from international sporting competitions. However, some athletes who compete as individuals without explicitly representing Russia, such as in cycling and tennis, have not been sanctioned, while other disciplines, such as biathlon or athletics, have suffered significant impacts.

Act II: With Paris 2024 Just One Year Away, the IOC Authorizes the Reinstatement of Russian Athletes, Under a Neutral Banner

Nevertheless, in 2023, just a few months before the Paris Games, the IOC was faced with the question of the participation of Russian and Belarusian athletes. Reflecting developments in international condemnation of Russian aggression and Russia's growing influence in Africa and Asia, the Asian Olympic Council and 54 African Olympic Committees supported the reinstatement, reflecting a trend towards a return to non-alignment on the part of certain countries in the Russian-Ukrainian conflict. The IOC must also respect its Olympic Charter, notably that athletes must not be sanctioned for the actions of their government (although the links between sport and politics are extremely close in Russia).

---

62. RODCHENKOV Grigory, *Dopage organisé*, Michel Lafon, 2021.

On March 28, 2023, the Olympic body reacted by proposing to reinstate Russian and Belarusian athletes in international competitions, subject to certain strict conditions: participation only under a neutral banner and in an individual capacity. The IOC added two conditions to take account of the Russian-Ukrainian conflict: the athletes must not publicly support the war or be under contract with their country's armed forces, since many Russian athletes are affiliated with the CSKA omnisports club, which has links with the army, and they must meet all anti-doping requirements[63]. A cautious reaction from the IOC at the time, to prepare the ground for a final decision on Paris 2024.

Indeed, the Olympic organization faces a dilemma following its political decision in February 2022. On the one hand, allowing Russian and Belarusian athletes to take part in the Games could be seen as a concession to Russia, which would be an affront to Ukraine and a significant part of the Western world, including many influential sports federations. On the other hand, if the IOC were to maintain its exclusion of these athletes, it could provoke opposition from the non-Western Olympic world, particularly given the explicit support of the African and Asian committees for their reinstatement, and call into question the principle of political neutrality promoted by the Olympic Charter.

---

63. IOC, "Recommendations on the participation of athletes holding a Russian or Belarusian passport in international competitions", March 28, 2023.

Act III: Russian Athletes' Participation Under Scrutiny as Ukraine Threatens Boycott

After a period of testing and deliberation on the reintegration of Russian athletes into the world sporting fold, it was on December 8, 2023 that the IOC officially took the decision to allow them to take part in Paris 2024, preserving the previously stated conditions. The Olympic body prepares the ground to avoid any political instrumentalization of Russian athletes, even under a neutral banner, with the drafting of a document detailing the "Principles relating to the implementation of the conditions for the participation of neutral individual athletes and their support staff holding a Russian or Belarusian passport in the Paris 2024 Olympic Games"[64].

These principles prohibit athletes from displaying the flags or emblems of their country or national committee, or any other symbol referring to the war in Ukraine, such as the Z symbol or the colors of St. George, the symbol of Russian patriotism. Official uniforms will be unicolored and, during medal ceremonies, the Russian or Belarusian anthems will be replaced by a neutral piece of music, which will not be the Olympic anthem. No team participation will be allowed for these athletes. Athletes will march under the flag of neutral individual athletes (AIN), designed specifically to avoid any national connotations. Medals won by NIAs will not be counted in the NOCs' official medal tables, and they will not take part in the parade of delegations at the opening ceremony[65].

---

64. IOC, "IOC Executive Board admits neutral individual athletes to Paris 2024 Olympic Games and imposes strict admission conditions", December 8, 2023.
65. "Paris 2024: the Court of Arbitration for Sport confirms the IOC's suspension of the Russian Olympic Committee", *Le Monde*, February 23, 2024.

This strictly neutral approach is in line with the sanctions imposed following the doping scandal, where Russia had already competed under the banner of the ROC (Russian Olympic Committee) at the Tokyo 2021 Games, but with many symbols that made this neutrality obsolete.

Russia will therefore have no visual presence at the Paris Games. The Russian National Olympic Committee will also not be invited, as it was suspended by the IOC in October 2023. The Russian NOC integrated four Ukrainian sports organizations, following Russia's unilateral annexation of the Ukrainian regions of Donetsk, Lugansk, Zaporijjia and Kherson in September 2022. Sporting integration was thus intended to further legitimize the annexation of these Ukrainian territories within Russia. Nevertheless, this violation of the territorial integrity of the National Olympic Committee of Ukraine falls within the scope of sport, and violates the Olympic Charter. This led to the IOC's decision to exclude the Russian NOC, confirmed by the Court of Arbitration for Sport (CAS) on February 23, 2024.

Is a Boycott of Ukraine Possible?

De facto, the IOC is still in a delicate position, juggling between its desire to maintain the universality of sport and its political neutrality, while at the same time maintaining sanctions against athletes as a result of geopolitical conflict. Faced with the IOC's changing position, Ukraine raised the possibility of a boycott of the Games. A threat taken seriously, since it could rally some of its allies. However, the great Olympic boycotts of 1980 and 1984 were strong political gestures, but this means of protest is now a thing of the past.

The global media platform represented by the Games, seen by more than half the planet, makes a boycott less impactful than active participation. An absence would be less effective than a well-orchestrated presence. Since the publication of the IOC's conditions for the limited participation of Russian athletes, the idea of a Ukrainian boycott seems to have been ruled out for the time being. Ukraine's visibility, with its flag, its symbols and a large delegation of athletes, sends a powerful message: despite Russian attempts at annexation, Ukrainian identity and sovereignty remain asserted and visible on the world stage.

The impact of sport is reflected in the reaction of Volodymyr Zelensky, President of Ukraine, when the Ukrainian national team qualified for Euro 2024: "Thanks guys! Thanks to the team! For the great emotions offered to the whole country. Thank you for demonstrating once again that every time Ukrainians face difficulties but don't give up and continue the fight, Ukrainians win. At a time when the enemy is trying to destroy us, we are proving every day that Ukrainians are and will remain. Ukraine is and will remain! Glory to Ukraine! As at the Euro soccer tournament, the Ukrainian athletes at the Paris Games will have a role far more than sporting. The Ukrainian presence, and any victories, will be a form of resistance and strong symbols of the Ukrainian nation's struggle in the face of Russia's war of aggression.

The Battle of Sport Continues for Vladimir Putin

In the face of multiple international sports sanctions, Vladimir Putin's Russia is trying to reintegrate world sport by reshuffling the deck. Sport, long a key element in Russian politics, is becoming an alternative battleground. Since participation in the Olympic Games is restricted, Putin is seeking to create an alternative, recalling the Friendship Games organized by the USSR in 1984 in response to the Soviet boycott of the Los Angeles Games[66]. This is in keeping with the Soviet tradition during the Cold War, and is intended to mark an even more pronounced break with the West[67].

As it stands, the IOC cannot prohibit the creation of these alternative sporting events, as sport itself cannot be "owned" by an entity. Only the Olympic symbols and marks are protected. Events such as the Commonwealth Games, the Jeux de la Francophonie and the Bolivarian Games already exist as recognized alternatives. Nevertheless, the IOC has expressed reservations about the motivations behind these "Friendship Games" planned for September 2024 and the "Winter Friendship Games" in 2026, calling them attempts to "politicize sport". The IOC criticizes Russia's aggressive approach, which, through an intense diplomatic offensive, seeks to convince world governments to participate in these Games for political purposes.

The Olympic body goes even further, calling on all stakeholders in the Olympic movement and all governments to reject any participation in, or support for, any initiative aimed at totally politicizing international sport, with the Friendship Games in its sights[68]. According to the Russian authorities, these Games are expected to bring together some 6,500 athletes and 70 countries, compared with the 10,500 athletes and over 200 national delegations expected at

---

66. Dufraisse Sylvain, *Une histoire sportive de la guerre froide,* Nouveau Monde Éditions, 2023.

67. Aubin Lukas, "Jeux de l'amitié en Russie : 'Un instrument de la guerre de Poutine contre l'Occident'", *La Croix,* April 9, 2024.

68. IOC, "IOC statement against the politicization of sport", March 19, 2024.

the Paris Games. The participation of nations in such a competition would have much more at stake than sport, as it would become part of Russia's game of influence. These "counter-games" are therefore to be seen as a new strategy by Putin in his war of influence against the West to reshape global geopolitical dynamics, using modern sport as a new weapon.

CHAPTER 18 - PARIS 2024: ISRAEL-PALESTINE

In the wake of the Russian-Ukrainian question, the Israeli-Palestinian conflict is also proving central to the Paris Olympic Games, given the tense geopolitical context between the two sides. This conflict flared up once again when the Hamas terrorist group launched a surprise attack in southern Israel on October 7, 2023, taking Israeli civilians hostage. In retaliation, the Israeli army launched a series of massive aerial bombardments, followed by a full-scale ground invasion of the Gaza Strip on October 27. Hostilities also extended to the occupied West Bank and along the border with Lebanon's Hezbollah. This latest escalation, the fifth war between Gaza and Israel since 2008, marks the most significant military confrontation in the region since the Yom Kippur War fifty years ago. The humanitarian consequences of these actions, and in particular the impact of the Israeli offensive in the Gaza Strip, have plunged the international community into deep uncertainty. The world stage offered by the Olympic Games will be particularly closely scrutinized, especially the participation of the Israeli and Palestinian delegations.

The Genesis of the Israeli-Palestinian Conflict

It would take much more than a single chapter to summarize the context of the Israeli-Palestinian conflict[69]. It is taking place in a land steeped in history, where religious, cultural and nationalist issues have been intertwined for millennia. Located at the crossroads of the Asian, African and European continents, this region has been the scene of incessant power struggles, largely due to its strategic position and spiritual importance for monotheistic religions, hosting some of the holiest sites of Judaism, Christianity and Islam. The origins of these tensions can be traced back to the late 19th century. At that time, in reaction to the rising anti-Semitism in Europe, the Zionist movement emerged. Promoted in particular by Theodor Herzl at a first congress in Basel, Switzerland, in 1897, it aimed to establish a Jewish national home in Palestine, a territory that had been under Ottoman rule since the 16th century[70].

The Sykes-Picot agreements, signed in 1916, were to reshuffle the cards. These agreements aimed to share areas of influence and control over the territories of the Ottoman Empire in the Middle East, anticipating its eventual dismemberment after the end of the First World War. These divisions, irrespective of existing ethnic or confessional boundaries, led to the partition of the region between France and the United Kingdom, and Palestine came under the British Mandate. In 1917, the Balfour Declaration (named after Arthur Balfour, British Secretary of State for Foreign Affairs) added to the context of the region, promising a "national home for the

---

69. Lemire Vincent, Snégaroff Thomas, *Israël/Palestine : anatomie d'un conflit*, Les Arènes, 2024.
70. Bensoussan Georges, *Les Origines du conflit israélo-arabe (1870-1950)*, PUF, coll. Que sais-je ?, 2023.

Jewish people" in Palestine. After the First World War, some 35,000 Jews emigrated to Palestine in response to post-war unrest and the lure of a promised Jewish national home. Several waves of Jewish immigration, known as "Aliyah", continued through the 1920s and accelerated in the 1930s as a result of Jewish persecution in Europe, particularly by the Nazi regime. The lack of concrete measures on the part of the British to bring these populations together led to the Great Arab Revolt of 1936-1939 in Palestine, which demanded an end to the British Mandate, the creation of an independent Arab state and an end to Jewish immigration.

The Second World War marked a relative pause in the nascent beginnings of this conflict. With the United Kingdom planning to relinquish its mandate over Palestine by 1948, the newly-formed United Nations (UN) attempted to bring peace to the region by proposing a partition of Palestine: a Jewish state, an Arab state and an international zone around Jerusalem and Bethlehem. Resolution no. 181 of November 29, 1947 was passed by 33 countries out of a total of 56 represented, but did not go down well with the main parties concerned. David Ben-Gurion's unilateral declaration of independence of the State of Israel on May 14, 1948 led to a reaction from neighboring Arab states and the 1948-1949 Arab-Israeli War. Israel emerged victorious, with an enlarged territory that led to the flight and expulsion of some 700,000 Palestinians, an event dubbed the "Nakba", or disaster in Arabic[71].

---

71. WEINSTOCK Nathan, *Terre promise, trop promise. Genèse du conflit israé-lo-palestinien (1882-1948)*, Odile Jacob, 2011.

After the Oslo Accords, a conflict still unresolved

The following decades were marked by several low- to high-intensity conflicts, including the Six-Day War in 1967 and the Yom Kippur War in 1973. Each of these wars had far-reaching consequences for the region, consolidating Israeli control over the disputed territories as well as the occupied territories of Gaza and the West Bank, and exacerbating the situation of the Palestinians. Attempts at peace, such as the 1979 Camp David Accords, have nevertheless shown moments of progress towards a resolution, but the process is often hampered by violence and political instability on both sides. The Oslo Accords, signed on September 13, 1993 under the aegis of the United States between Israeli Prime Minister Yitzhak Rabin and PLO (Palestine Liberation Organization) leader Yasser Arafat, were nevertheless a beacon of hope. They paved the way for a bilateral dialogue between the two parties, and for the creation of the Palestinian National Authority, charged with running a limited Palestinian autonomy over parts of the West Bank and Gaza Strip, leaving the door open to the future creation of a Palestinian state. Unfortunately, the hostility between the two sides continued unabated, and the assassination of Yitzhak Rabin in 1995 by a far-right Israeli student stalled the peace process that had been initiated, and hopes of a lasting resolution to tensions faded with time[72].

The conflict remains intensely complex, with periodic cycles of violence and sporadic attempts at negotiation. The recognition of the State of Palestine by the UN in 2012 as a "non-member observer state" is a symbolic step, but on the ground, the status quo persists,

---

72. DIECKHOFF Alain, *Israël-Palestine : une guerre sans fin*, Armand Colin, 2022.

complicated by international politics and regional alliances. The peace process remains at a standstill. Internal Palestinian divisions and continued Israeli colonization of the Palestinian territory of the West Bank exacerbate tensions. The Abraham Accords, signed on May 13, 2020, by which certain Arab states normalized their relations with Israel, are also indicative of a relative abandonment of the Palestinian cause by the Arab world, leaving the field open for extremist organizations such as Hamas to carry the fight forward.

Munich 1972: When the Israeli-Palestinian Conflict Tragically Enters the Olympic Context

The Olympic movement was also involved in this conflict, since a sporting event such as the Olympic Games is so symbolic for a state in terms of its international legitimacy. At the 1948 Olympic Games, for example, the newly-formed State of Israel asked the IOC to take part in the Parade of Nations, but the IOC refused, as Israel had no official recognition at the time and this could have led to a massive boycott by Arab countries. The issue remained unresolved at the 1952 Helsinki Games, with intense debate surrounding recognition of Israel's NOC. It was finally accepted by the IOC, enabling the Hebrew state to send a delegation of athletes to the Games for the first time.

While no country boycotts were recorded following Israel's participation, the Israeli-Palestinian conflict was to reverberate with great violence during the Munich Olympics. On September 5, 1972, members of Septembre Noir, a terrorist organization affiliated to the PLO, scaled the fences of the Olympic Village and burst into the Israeli team's quarters. They took eleven members of the Israeli delegation of athletes and coaches hostage, in an attack designed to draw worldwide attention to the Palestinian cause. The attack was deeply rooted in regional tensions exacerbated by the 1967 Six-Day War, during which Israel took control of the West Bank, Gaza, the Sinai Peninsula and the Golan Heights. This significantly increased friction in the region, including reprisals by Palestinian independence groups and other Arab movements[73].

In the first few hours, the terrorists killed two members of the Israeli delegation who tried to resist. The other nine hostages were held in the hope of exchanging their release for that of 234 Palestinian prisoners held in Israel, as well as other radical figures imprisoned in Europe. The Israeli government, refusing to negotiate with the terrorists, watched the situation unfold, while the German authorities tried to manage the crisis. The tragedy culminates in a poorly negotiated rescue attempt at Fürstenfeldbruck airport. The operation, marked by tactical errors and lack of preparation, culminates in a bloody shootout in which all nine Israeli hostages are killed, along with five of the eight members of the terrorist commando and a German policeman.

The Munich bombing in 1972 marked a tragic turning point in Olympic history: it was the first time that the Games were interrupted due to an act of terrorism. The tragedy immediately highlighted the security shortcomings of international sporting events. Previously, the Games had been seen as an apolitical celebration of sport and the human spirit, but Munich exposed their vulnerability to global political issues. In subsequent editions, notably starting with the Montreal Games in 1976, greater emphasis was placed on

---

73. WAWRZYNIAK Richard, *Histoire(s) des Jeux olympiques*, Mareuil Éditions, 2021.

security, transforming the Olympic villages into guarded fortresses and permanently altering the Games experience for athletes and spectators alike. In addition, this attack raises questions about the IOC's response to political issues within its flagship event. The main criticism concerns the IOC's controversial decision to continue the Games after a single day of mourning. Avery Brundage, then President of the IOC and a fervent advocate of apolitical sport, symbolized the Olympic body's firm line: "The Games must go on!"

Paris 2024: Israel and Palestine Take Center Stage

Now, in 2024, the Olympic body has evolved to take account of the geopolitical climate, while trying to preserve the political neutrality of the Olympic movement. And yet, despite the absence of a Palestinian state, the sporting arena remains one of the few places where Palestine is represented in the same way as other states. Not least in the Olympic movement, since the optimism displayed following the Oslo Accords led to the recognition by the IOC in 1995 of the Palestinian National Olympic Committee, created in 1986. Palestine's first official participation in the Olympic Games took place a year later at the Atlanta Games, marking a historic moment. Majed Abu Marahil, proudly carrying the Palestinian flag at the opening ceremony, symbolized Palestine's entry into the international arena of sport and as a national entity in contact with other nations.

Since Atlanta, only 25 Palestinian athletes have represented Palestine. For the Paris Olympics, the participation of Palestinian athletes will once again be more than limited. For Jibril Rajoub, President of the Palestine Olympic Committee, "the recent Israeli military operations have brought youth and sport in Palestine to their knees." According to him, "more than a thousand people have already been killed among members of youth, sports and scouting organizations"[74]. In this delicate position, the IOC is trying to maintain its position of neutrality while assuring that it will continue "to assist as much as possible the Palestinian NOC and its athletes in their preparation and qualification for the Paris 2024 Olympic Games"[75].

The participation of Palestinian and Israeli delegations in Paris 2024 will be particularly scrutinized, as these athletes are perceived as ambassadors for their respective countries. The IOC has to play a delicate diplomatic game. It cannot respond to certain calls for Israel's exclusion from the Games, as the Israeli NOC has not violated the Olympic Charter and the various member NOCs are not calling for Israel's exclusion. The IOC cannot therefore act outside its sphere of competence, even though pressure is mounting from certain countries to condemn Israel's military actions in Palestine. On May 21, 2024, Spain, Slovenia and Norway announced their intention to officially recognize the Palestinian state, a symbolic but powerful step towards a diplomatic solution and pressure on Israel to end its offensive.

Paris 2024 promises to be an arena where sporting and political issues will be closely intertwined. The IOC, while supporting Palestinian participation, will have to maneuver carefully to maintain the neutrality and unity of the Olympic movement in the face of growing international pressure and geopolitical tensions.

---

74. ACHACHE Farid, « La présence de la Palestine aux JO de Paris en 2024 en question », *RFI*, January 4, 2024.
75. IOC, "IOC President welcomes Palestinian NOC to Olympic House", April 18, 2024.

CHAPTER 19: BERMUDA, FIJI, JAMAICA, KENYA... THE OLYMPIC GAMES: SHOWCASING NATIONS

The world geopolitical map and the Olympic map don't always coincide. Indeed, the IOC now has more member countries (206) than the UN (193), illustrating how sport can transcend traditional political divisions. This can be seen at the Olympic Games, which provide an international platform for national entities that might otherwise remain invisible or marginalized on the world stage. We have seen this in the cases of Kosovo, Hong Kong and Palestine. Numerous other examples testify to Olympism's ability to build bridges and reveal little-known nations.

Non-Independent Countries at the Olympics

First of all, it should be remembered that it is the National Olympic Committees (NOCs) that are responsible for representing their countries at the Olympic Games, and not the States themselves. To take part in the Olympic Games, an NOC must be recognized by the IOC. This recognition is based on several criteria, including compliance with the principles of the Olympic Charter, commitment to promoting the values of Olympism, independence from political authorities and democratic operation. Until the 1990s, the IOC applied relatively flexible rules to NOC recognition for dependent territories and constituent countries. These territories could be recognized as separate entities within the IOC, even if they were not recognized as independent countries by the international community.

The geopolitical upheavals brought about by the end of the Cold War and the collapse of the Eastern bloc created a dynamic in which many newly independent states sought international recognition through membership of international organizations. For some countries, having their NOC recognized by the IOC and the prospect of parading their national symbols in a mondovision ceremony is a strategic priority.

In 1996, the Olympic body adapted its rules to meet these new geopolitical realities. The amendment introduces a change: for a territory to be recognized as an NOC by the IOC, it must first be recognized as an independent country by the international community. This criterion remains relatively vague. It means that territories and entities can no longer automatically create separate NOCs if they do not meet this international recognition criterion. However, this criterion can sometimes be open to debate, as demonstrated by the case of Kosovo. In 2014, despite partial international recognition, Kosovo, a non-member of the UN, was accepted as a full member of the IOC, allowing its athletes to compete under their own flag at the 2016 Rio Games[76].

---

76. For further details, see chapter 16 on Olympic recognition of Kosovo.

However, these criteria are not retroactive, which means that some countries that are not officially independent can still compete in the Olympic Games, since their NOC was recognized before the reform. This is particularly true of Puerto Rico. Although an unincorporated territory of the United States, it has its own NOC and has been competing at the Games under its own flag since 1948, thanks to a significant degree of autonomy that enables it to regulate its own Olympic movement, irrespective of its political status. Puerto Rico has even won gold medals thanks to Mónica Puig in tennis (Rio 2016) and Jasmine Camacho-Quinn (Tokyo 2021). Aruba, meanwhile, established its own Olympic Committee in 1986, shortly after obtaining its status as a "constituent country" of the Kingdom of the Netherlands. Bermuda, a British overseas territory with extended responsibilities, and the Cook Islands, a state in free association with New Zealand, also have their own NOCs, underlining their ability to promote sport independently of their wider political status. Bermuda, with its 60,000 inhabitants, is the smallest country in terms of population to have won a gold medal, thanks to Flora Duffy in triathlon (Tokyo 2021). Other examples, such as the U.S. Virgin Islands and the British Virgin Islands, also illustrate this point, which is why we see the colors of these non-independent countries in the parade of nations at the traditional opening ceremony of the Games.

"Micro-States" at the Heart of the Olympic Games

The Olympics also serve as a global showcase for countries which, because of their size or limited population, have difficulty establishing themselves on the international stage. Micro-states such as Monaco (1920[77]), Liechtenstein (1936), San Marino (1960) and Andorra (1976) have seized this opportunity to assert their identity and global presence. Although winning medals may be a rarity for these small countries, the interest lies elsewhere, since participation is already seen as a victory. Nevertheless, some delegations stood out.

At the Tokyo 2021 Olympic Games, San Marino, one of the world's smallest republics (61 km^2), managed to win a silver medal in shooting and two bronze in wrestling, making history as the smallest nation to win so many medals at a single edition of the Games. This exceptional performance not only put San Marino in the international spotlight, but also demonstrated how the Games can be the stage for feats, no matter how powerful the participating country.

The Participation of Oceania's Island Countries: A Forum to Raise Awareness of Global Warming

In addition to European micro-states, the Olympic Games are also showcasing other "little ones": the island countries of Oceania, a region where many nations see their existence threatened by global warming and rising sea levels. Countries such as Nauru, Tuvalu and the Marshall Islands, tiny on a global scale, are using their participation as an international platform to raise the alarm about climate change. The most notable example is undoubtedly Tonga. Athlete Pita Taufatofua drew worldwide attention during

---

77. The dates correspond to the first participation of the NOCs of these countries in the Olympic Games.

the opening ceremonies of the Rio 2016 Olympic Games by parading shirtless, body oiled, wearing traditional Tongan costume. This gesture not only showcased her country's culture, but also drew attention to Tonga, a small Polynesian kingdom of 100,000 inhabitants that faces significant environmental risks. Taufatofua repeated this appearance at the Tokyo 2021 Games and, more surprisingly, at the 2018 Winter Olympics in Pyeonchang, consolidating her status as a cultural icon and unwitting spokesperson for the climate issues affecting the Pacific islands.

Among these island states, Fiji has particularly stood out in recent years. The reintroduction of rugby sevens at the Rio Olympics in 2016 offered a unique opportunity for Fiji and its 900,000 inhabitants to demonstrate their talent in this sport to the world. Rugby has been deeply rooted in Fijian culture since the late 19th century. The sport, with its physical contact and values, is in keeping with local customs and ancient avoidance games of the indigenous people, such as *veibona* (a kind of cat-and-mouse game). Thanks to their rugby sevens team, Fiji shone in Rio, winning their first-ever gold medal. This title will be confirmed again in 2021 at the Tokyo Olympics. These Olympic victories have reinforced their status as an established rugby nation. The *Flying Fijians'* performances in Rio and Tokyo, as well as their emotional celebration, have captured the world's attention.

Jamaica, Kenya, Cuba...: Sports Specialization as a Driver of Medals and Visibility

The Olympic Games also serve as a global showcase for nations excelling in specific disciplines. This specialization enables countries with relatively low profile or smaller delegations to compete for medals against established Olympic nations. Countries such as Jamaica, Kenya and Cuba have exploited their excellence in certain disciplines not only to strengthen their international presence, but also to enhance their country's international image through sport.

Jamaica has made Olympic history thanks to its exceptional sprinters. Particularly Usain Bolt, who consolidated Jamaica's image as the home of the world's fastest sprinters. His performance in Beijing in 2008, where he broke the 100 m and 200 m world records, and the confirmation of his performances in London in 2012 and Rio in 2016, with 8 medals in total and all gold, not only transformed athletics, but also elevated Jamaica's global status. The impact of these athletes on the international perception of Jamaica is profound, making the country a benchmark of world sprinting and sporting success.

Kenya and Ethiopia are renowned for their domination of long-distance races. One image in particular illustrates this during one of Ethiopia's first participations. At the 1960 Olympic Games in Rome, Ethiopia's Abebe Bikila won the barefoot marathon and became the first black African Olympic champion. The successes have continued ever since, and Kenya has also invited itself into the dance of these disciplines. Figures such as Eliud Kipchoge for Kenya and Kenenisa Bekele for Ethiopia are emblematic examples who not only won gold medals, but also shaped the image of their countries as the long-distance running capitals of the world. Kipchoge's

Olympic victories, notably in 2016 and 2021, and Bekele's historic successes in 2004 and 2008, have positioned their nations. Ethiopia has even won all 58 of its Olympic medals in cross-country and middle-distance running.

Cuba is famous for its excellent boxers such as Teófilo Stevenson and Félix Savón, whose multiple Olympic victories (three gold medals each) have highlighted the strength of the Cuban boxing program. These sporting successes are closely linked to the geopolitical context and Fidel Castro's regime. After the 1959 revolution, the Castro regime used sport, and boxing in particular, as a propaganda tool to promote socialist ideals and demonstrate the superiority of their system over capitalist nations, particularly the United States. The Cuban sports program, strongly supported by the state, created development academies for athletes, integrating party ideology into sports training, and offering free education and health care to athletes. As a result, the Castro model has gained international recognition thanks to the performances of its athletes. Cuba's total medal tally for the Games was 235, placing it 20th in the world.

Other more recently independent countries have turned to sporting specialization. Like Mongolia, with its deeply-rooted wrestling traditions, which has used its skills in this specific discipline, as well as in boxing and judo, to win medals. The 2008 Olympic gold medals won by judoka Naidangiin Tüvshinbayar and boxer Enkhbatyn Badar-Uugan not only brought medals, but also highlighted Mongolia's rich cultural heritage in combat sports. The world's largest landlocked country, with a population of just 3 million, now boasts 30 Olympic medals. Since its first participation as an independent nation in 1996, Kazakhstan has also chosen to specialize in the strength disciplines of boxing, wrestling and weightlifting. Boxing in particular, with Kazakh athletes winning 24 of the 79 medals won in this sport. This has helped shape Kazakhstan's international image as a strong, competitive nation in these demanding disciplines.

Through sporting specialization, nations that don't have the full range of infrastructures, or that have smaller populations than the "sporting giants", can succeed in distinguishing themselves in specific disciplines. And thus succeed in capturing Olympic performance, so that their country can be recognized on the world map by billions of television viewers[78].

---

78. To find out more, Augustin Jean-Pierre, Gillon Pascal, *Les jeux du monde. Géopolitique de la flamme olympique*, Armand Colin, 2021.

Chapter 20: Qatar, Saudi Arabia, India... Towards New Olympic Horizons?

Today, the Olympic Games represent much more than the simple organization of a major international sporting event; they are a symbol of prestige and an instrument for demonstrating a country's power on the world stage. Historically created, organized and dominated by Western nations, the Games have gradually evolved to reflect a more diverse geopolitical landscape[79]. A significant shift took place in 2008, when the Beijing Games served as a showcase for China's economic rise and commitment to modernization. This marked a turning point, showing how an emerging country can use the Games to amplify its international stature in the face of the great powers, notably the United States.

Since then, rising powers have also become Olympic hosts, such as Russia with the Sochi Winter Games in 2014 and Brazil with the Rio Summer Games in 2016, helping to shift the Olympic center of gravity away from traditional Western strongholds. Despite a slowdown in the competition to host the 2024 and 2028 Games,

---

79. Augustin Jean-Pierre, Gillon Pascal, *Les jeux du monde. Géopolitique de la flamme olympique*, Armand Colin, 2021.

awarded respectively to Paris and Los Angeles for lack of other bids, the competition to stage one of the world's biggest sporting and media events is once again gathering pace. New emerging powers from the "Global South", in particular the BRICS+[80], are implementing genuine political strategies in which sport plays a central role. The aim is manifold: to attract international investors and tourists, develop their *soft power* and accentuate their *nationbranding*.

The West is no Longer the Center of Gravity at the Olympics

In recent decades, the interest of Western countries[81] in hosting the Olympic Games has waned considerably. Historically, the Games were often the preserve of Western nations, seen as an opportunity to demonstrate their supremacy, technological innovation and preserve a certain established world order. Between 1896 and 1991, 117 cities competed for the right to host the Olympic Games, including 64 European, 42 American, 5 Asian, 3 Oceanic and 3 African cities[82]. Economic and geopolitical realities have since evolved, allowing new powers (China, Brazil) to position themselves. The costs associated with organizing the modern Olympic Games since 2004 now range from 10 to 15 billion dollars (with the exception of the Beijing Games), not counting any additional costs, combined

---

80. BRICS+ is a geopolitical grouping of countries from the "Global South", including major emerging countries (Brazil, China, India) and regional powers (South Africa, Egypt, Iran, Russia, Saudi Arabia, United Arab Emirates).
81. By Western countries we mean North America, Europe and Australasia (Australia-New Zealand).
82. Aubin Lukas, Guégan Jean-Baptiste, *Atlas géopolitique du sport*, Autrement, 2022.

with the social and environmental impacts of certain editions. This has led to a reassessment of the value of the Olympics, and of the relevance of wanting to have an Olympic Games on home soil at all costs, particularly for the population of the host city.

A striking phenomenon of this disaffection is the multiplication of referendums within host cities, which have led to the withdrawal of certain bids. This was the case for the city of Hamburg in Germany for the 2024 Games, where in 2015, 51.6% of voters opposed the project, mainly due to concerns over financial costs and environmental consequences. Boston and Budapest also withdrew their bids in the face of public opposition. The situation for the 2024 and 2028 Games illustrates this change in dynamic. With only two candidate cities remaining (Paris and Los Angeles), the IOC took the unusual step of awarding each one an edition of the Games.

The growing importance of a sustainable legacy and environmental responsibility is now at the heart of Olympic bids. Host cities, such as Paris for the 2024 Olympics, are now assessed on their ability to ensure a positive legacy, fully integrate the local community into the benefits of the Games and reduce their ecological impact. These criteria reflect the IOC's new strategy, called "Olympic Agenda 2020+5", which serves as a roadmap for meeting these challenges and those of the post COVID-19 period. Brisbane, Australia, the host city for the 2032 Olympics, is proposing a project focused on sustainability, using existing infrastructure and minimizing new construction. Although the 2024, 2028 and 2032 editions were awarded to traditional countries with Olympic legacies and sports infrastructures, new countries had positioned themselves to host the 2032 Games before the COVID-19 crisis. India (Ahmedabad), Indonesia (Jakarta) and Qatar (Doha), not forgetting Saudi Arabia, are among the list of potential new candidates.

Qatar, Saudi Arabia: Political and Sporting Ambition from the Persian Gulf

The nations of the Persian Gulf, in particular Qatar, the United Arab Emirates and Saudi Arabia, are making considerable efforts to position themselves as new global sports centers. Their strategy is both political and sporting, and aims to diversify their economies—traditionally dependent on oil and gas revenues—and improve their international image. By hosting world-class sporting events, these countries aspire to a modern, international projection, while asserting that their countries are capable of organizing and hosting such competitions.

The best example of this strategy is Qatar. The small emirate of 2.8 million inhabitants has invested significantly in sport since 1995, to reveal itself to the world and break away from Saudi influence. This strategy, backed by gas revenues, has enabled Qatar to invest in a number of sporting fields (2006 Asian Games, purchase of PSG, BeIn Sports media network) and to integrate into sports decision-making bodies. The apotheosis of this plan will culminate in 2010 with the organization of the 2022 FIFA World Cup. Despite the controversy surrounding the ecological and human costs of this World Cup, Qatar has successfully demonstrated to the world that it is capable of organizing, hosting and overcoming the logistical and political challenges of a sporting mega-event[83]. All arguments that make the emirate, with its almost unlimited revenues and ambitions, a credible candidate to host the Olympic Games.

---

83. For more details, see my previous book on the Qatar-Saudi Arabia chapter, *Football Club Geopolitics. 22 histoires insolites pour comprendre le monde*, Max Milo, 2024.

Saudi Arabia, observing the successes of its Qatari rival, has stepped up its own investment in sport since Crown Prince Mohammed Ben Salmane came to power in 2015. Politically-motivated investments to accompany the Vision 2030 modernization plan and to improve the kingdom's overshadowed international image have been undertaken. Since 2018, the organization of events and investments in sport have continued apace: renowned boxing matches, the Dakar Rally, cycling races, the Formula 1 Grand Prix, substantial investments in golf and soccer (purchase of English club Newcastle, development of the "star league" Saudi Pro League, etc.). Saudi Pro League, etc.). As a regional power, Saudi Arabia is catching up with its rivals. The award of the 2029 Asian Winter Games and the 2034 FIFA World Cup confirm the kingdom's ambition to become a key player on the world sporting stage. The battle with Qatar for the Olympic Games has only just begun.

India, the "Sleeping Giant" in the Olympic Race

Beyond the Persian Gulf nations, other emerging powers are seeking to use the Olympic Games to assert a new international status and develop their *nationbranding*. India, as one of the world's fastest-growing economies and the world's new most populous country (1.43 billion inhabitants), is showing increased interest in the Olympics, not only as a means of reinforcing its international image, but also to confirm its role as an assertive power. With significant improvements in its sporting infrastructure and increased investment in athlete training, India has seen an increase in its Olympic successes. For example, at the Tokyo 2021 Olympic Games, Neeraj Chopra won the javelin throwing competition, marking a historic moment as India's first gold medal in athletics. The country now has a total of 7 medals from these Games, illustrating its growing competence and the efforts made by India to wake up this country often considered a "sleeping giant" on the sporting scene[84].

Indonesia, with its population of 270 million, also has ambitions to host an Olympiad. Following the successful organization of the 2018 Asian Games on its soil, President Joko Widodo announced that Jakarta would be a candidate for the 2032 edition. After the COVID-19 pandemic, ambitions remain intact. Nevertheless, a number of events, including the tragedy at Kanjuruhan stadium with its 174 deaths on November 16, 2022, and the cancellation of the 2023 FIFA U-20 Cup in favor of Argentina, because Indonesia did not want to host the Israeli team, have cast doubt on the ability of the country, home to the world's largest Muslim population, to organize a major international sporting event on the scale of the Olympics.

Africa's Chances?

Africa remains the continent that has never hosted an Olympic Games. So far, South Africa is the only African country to have hosted a sporting event of this scale, with the 2010 Football World Cup. Morocco will be the second to do so, but in a joint organization with Spain and Portugal, for the 2030 World Cup. These two African countries, along with Egypt, which is considering a bid for the 2036

---

84. BONIFACE Pascal, *Géopolitique du sport*, Dunod, 2023.

Olympics with the city of Cairo, remain the three African chances capable of putting forward a bid to attempt to host an Olympiad.

There's another player to keep an eye on: Senegal. Dakar will host the Youth Olympic Games in 2026. This event, the first of its kind on the African continent, is seen as a crucial stage in testing the Senegalese state's ability to manage large-scale events and showcase African sporting talent in this miniature re-run of the Olympics.

Globalization, Global Warming, Political Neutrality: The IOC's Future Challenges in the Face of these New Horizons

The IOC is at a significant strategic crossroads. In seeking to further universalize the Games, the Olympic body, with 206 member NOCs, is striving not to restrict the organization of the event to traditional nations. However, this necessary openness poses a major dilemma, particularly when the potential host countries do not fully share the values of Western democracies, as well as a certain respect for human rights, and may be governed by authoritarian regimes. This issue has become particularly topical in the wake of criticism and calls for boycotts of the FIFA 2022 World Cup in Qatar and the Beijing 2022 Winter Olympics.

For emerging powers aspiring to organize a sporting event on the scale of the Olympic Games, this means building multiple infrastructures to accommodate all sporting disciplines, as they cannot rely on pre-existing facilities. This imperative may conflict with the issues of sustainability and inclusion promoted by the IOC, creating a major challenge for these new candidates. The Paris 2024 Games are envisaged as a pioneering model in this new era, with a more controlled budget and a focus on legacy and ecological impact.

However, it is uncertain whether emerging powers will be willing or able to follow this model, especially if they want to invest massively to make their Olympics a mega-event with the aim of impressing the planet. At the end of the day, the IOC has a real role to play as an international player. It is engaged in a balancing act: it seeks to preserve the universalism of the "neutral" space that the Olympiads represent, while adapting them to international dynamics.

The Olympic Games therefore remain a global theater of nations, where not only sporting competitions are played out, but also the major issues of our time. They are a reflection of global tensions and aspirations, a place where sporting emotion and geopolitical challenges meet, making the Games a mirror of the complexities of our contemporary world.

ACKNOWLEDGEMENTS

A fourth book in four years deciphering geopolitical issues through sport... I wouldn't have believed it just a few years ago.

Once again, this latest book would never have seen the light of day if it hadn't been for the fierce passion for sport I've shared since childhood with my brother Anthony, with whom I've spent many hours watching France Télévisions so as not to miss a thing of the Olympic Games. A real gateway to my future interest in geography, history and politics. Many thanks to him.

Thanks to my other half, my wife Zoé, who has supported me throughout this fourth project with her joie de vivre and, perhaps most importantly, her love.

Thanks to my mother, Nadège, who has always supported me whatever my ideas, projects and obstacles.

Thank you to Jean-Charles Gérard, my publisher, for trusting me once again.

Thanks to my family, to all my friends and family. In particular, the proofreaders' club: Florian, François, Geoffrey, Guillaume M., Guillaume C., Jean-Luc, Mathieu, Romain, Sarah and Vincent.

Thank you to the 70,000 subscribers of FC Geopolitics, the media outlet I founded in November 2019, without whom this new literary adventure would not have been possible.

Finally, a thought for my wonderful grandmother Pierrette, and also for my grandfather Aurélio, who left too soon, who always hold a special place in my heart.

BIBLIOGRAPHY

Collective work, *Une histoire mondiale de l'olympisme : 1896-2024*, Atlande, 2023.

ANDERSON Benedict, *L'imaginaire national. Réflexions sur l'origine et l'essor du nationalisme*, La Découverte, 1996.

ARCHAMBAULT Fabien, *Les légendes du siècle. Une histoire des Jeux en douze médailles*, Flammarion, 2024.

AUBIN Lukas, *La sportokratura sous Vladimir Poutine*, Bréal, 2022.

AUBIN Lukas, GUÉGAN Jean-Baptiste, *Atlas géopolitique du sport*, Autrement, 2022.

AUGUSTIN Jean-Pierre, GILLON Pascal, *Les jeux du monde. Géopolitique de la flamme olympique*, Armand Colin, 2021.

BENSOUSSAN Georges, *Les Origines du conflit israélo-arabe (1870-1950)*, PUF, coll. Que sais-je ?, 2023.

BLAKEMORE Erin, "A Divided Germany Came Together for the Olympics Decades Before Korea Did", History.com, February 12, 2018.

BODIS Jean-Pierre, *Le rugby sud-africain. Histoire d'un sport en politique*, Karthala, 1995.

BONIFACE Pascal, *JO politiques*, Éditions Eyrolles, 2016.

Boniface Pascal, *Géopolitique du sport*, Dunod, 2023.

Boissonade Euloge, Charpentier Henri, *La grande histoire des Jeux olympiques*, France Empire, 1999.

Brohm Jean-Marie, *1936 : Les Jeux olympiques à Berlin*, André Versaille éditeur, 2008.

Budzier Alexander, Flyvbjerg Bent, Stewart Allison, "The Oxford Olympics Study 2016: Cost and Cost Overrun at the Games", University of Oxford, July 2016.

Burgan Michael, *Miracle on Ice: How a Stunning Upset United a Country*, Compass Point Books, 2016.

Caraccioli Tom, Caraccioli Jerry, *Boycott: Stolen Dreams of the 1980 Moscow Olympic Games*, New Chapter Press, 2008.

Cattaruzza Amaël, Sintès Pierre, *Atlas géopolitique des Balkans*, Autrement, 2016.

Chadwick Simon, Widdop Paul, Goldman Michael, *The Geopolitical Economy of Sport*, Routledge, 2023.

Clastres Patrick, *Jeux Olympiques, un siècle de passions*, Les quatre Chemins, 2008.

Coubertin Pierre de, *Les batailles de l'éducation physique. Une campagne de vingt-et-un ans (1887-1908)*, Paris, Librairie de l'Éducation physique, 1909.

Coubertin Pierre de, *Mémoires olympiques*, Bartillat, 2016.

Dieckhoff Alain, *Israël-Palestine : une guerre sans fin ?*, Armand Colin, 2022.

Dufraisse Sylvain, *Une histoire sportive de la guerre froide*, Nouveau Monde Éditions, 2023.

Dufraisse Sylvain, *Les héros du sport. Une histoire des champions soviétiques (années 1930-années 1980)*, Champ Vallon, 2019.

Dunning Eric, Elias Norbert, *Sport et civilisation*, Fayard, 1994.

GYGAX Jérôme, *Olympisme et guerre froide culturelle. Le prix de la victoire américaine*, L'Harmattan, 2012.

GUEGAN Jean-Baptiste, *Géopolitique du sport. Une autre explication du monde*, Bréal, 2022.

GUOQUI XU, *Olympic Dreams: China and Sports, 1895-2008*, Harvard University Press, 2008.

KESSOUS Mustapha, *Les 100 histoires des Jeux olympiques*, PUF, Que sais-je ? series, 2012.

LAMBROS Spyridon and POLITES Nikolas G., « Rapport officiel des Jeux olympiques de 1896 ».

LEMIRE Vincent, SNÉGAROFF Thomas, *Israël/Palestine : anatomie d'un conflit*, Les Arènes, 2024.

MARTINEZ-DELCAYROU Thibaut, *Faute ! Dans les coulisses des plus grandes polémiques arbitrales*, Hugo Sport, 2022.

MONNIN Éric and MONNIN Catherine, « Le boycott politique des Jeux olympiques de Montréal », *Relations internationales*, 2008/2 (n° 134).

OLARU Stejarel, *Nadia Comaneci dans l'œil de la police secrète*, Robert Laffont, 2022.

Revue Hérodote, *Géopolitique de l'Olympisme*, La Découverte, 2024.

RODCHENKOV Grigory, *Dopage organisé*, Michel Lafon, 2021.

TERRET Thierry, *Histoire du sport*, PUF, coll. Que sais-je ?, 2013.

THILOU Thomas, *Histoire(s) de Jeux : Les Jeux Olympiques de 1896 à 2021, 125 ans d'Humanité*, L'Harmattan, 2022.

THOMAZEAU François, *Histoire secrète du sport*, La Découverte, 2019.

TRÉGOURÈS Loïc, *Le football et le chaos yougoslave*, Non Lieu, 2019.

VEYSSIÈRE Kévin, *Football Club Geopolitics. 22 histoires insolites pour comprendre le monde*, Max Milo, new edition, 2024.

VEYSSIÈRE Kévin, *Football Club Geopolitics. Mondial : 22 histoires insolites sur la Coupe du monde de football*, Max Milo, 2022.

VEYSSIÈRE Kévin, *Planète Rugby : 50 questions géopolitiques*, Max Milo, 2023.

WAWRZYNIAK Richard, *Histoire(s) des Jeux olympiques*, Mareuil Éditions, 2021.

WEINSTOCK Nathan, *Terre promise, trop promise. Genèse du conflit israélo-palestinien (1882-1948)*, Odile Jacob, 2011.

WERNICKE Luciano, *Les histoires insolites des Jeux olympiques d'été*, Amphora, 2020.

Table of Contents

Introduction 7

Chapter 1: The Geopolitical Origins of the Olympic Games 13

Chapter 2 - 1896 Athens: The First Games in the Service
of the New Greek State 21

Chapter 3 - 1912 Stockholm - 1920 Antwerp:
Impossible Olympic Neutrality................................29

Chapter 4 - 1936 Berlin: Using the Olympic Games
to Further Nazi Ideology 37

Chapter 5 - 1940 Tokyo - Helsinki: The Impossible Games.......45

Chapter 6 - 1952 Helsinki: From the "Cold War"
to the "Medal War" 51

Chapter 7 - 1956 Melbourne: From the Suez Crisis
to the "Bloodbath" 59

Chapter 8 - 1968 Mexico: Beyond the Raised Fists 67

Chapter 9 - 1972 Munich: The Paradox of the Two Germanys.... 75

Chapter 10 - 1976 Montreal: Apartheid: The First Major
Boycott of the Olympic Games 83

Chapter 1 - 1980 Moscow - 1984 Los Angeles:
Boycott *vs.* Boycott: The Olympic Games
at the Center of the Cold War 91

Chapter 12 - 1992 Barcelona: The Games
of "Reconciliation"? 103

Chapter 13 - Sydney 2000: Aborigines and Unified Korea:
A New Dimension for the Opening Ceremony 111

Chapter 14 - Beijing 2008: Demonstrating Chinese
Superpower 117

Chapter 15 - 2016 - Rio: Olympic Recognition for Kosovo 125

Chapter 16 - Paris 2024: A Geopolitical Challenge for France .. 133

Chapter 17 - Paris 2024: Russia-Ukraine 141

Chapter 18 - Paris 2024: Israel-Palestine 151

Chapter 19: Bermuda, Fiji, Jamaica, Kenya...
The Olympic Games: Showcasing Nations 159

Chapter 20: Qatar, Saudi Arabia, India...
Towards New Olympic Horizons? 167

Acknowledgements 175

Bibliography 177

Best sellers Max Milo Editions

Hitler's banker, Jean-François Bouchard

Confessions of a forger, Éric Piedoie Le Tiec

The Koran and the flesh, Ludovic-Mohamed Zahed

Governing by fake news, Jacques Baud

Governing by chaos, Lucien Cerise

A political history of food, Paul Ariès

Mad in U.S.A.: The ravages of the "American model",
Michel Desmurget

Mondial soccer club geopolitics, Kévin Veyssière

Putin: Game master?, Jacques Baud

Treatise on the three impostors: Moses, Jesus, Muhammad,
The Spirit of Spinoza

TV Lobotomy, Michel Desmurget

The Russian Art of War: How the West Led Ukraine to Defeat,
Jacques Baud